ANCIENT PHILOSOPHY

FROM 600 BCE TO 500 CE

The History of Philosophy

ANCIENT PHILOSOPHY

FROM 600 BCE TO 500 CE

EDITED BY BRIAN DUIGNAN, SENIOR EDITOR,
PHILOSOPHY AND RELIGION

Britannica®
Educational Publishing

IN ASSOCIATION WITH

ROSEN
EDUCATIONAL SERVICES

Published in 2011 by Britannica Educational Publishing
(a trademark of Encyclopædia Britannica, Inc.)
in association with Rosen Educational Services, LLC
29 East 21st Street, New York, NY 10010.

First Edition

Britannica Educational Publishing
Michael I. Levy: Executive Editor
J.E. Luebering: Senior Manager
Marilyn L. Barton: Senior Coordinator, Production Control
Steven Bosco: Director, Editorial Technologies
Lisa S. Braucher: Senior Producer and Data Editor
Yvette Charboneau: Senior Copy Editor
Kathy Nakamura: Manager, Media Acquisition
Brian Duignan: Senior Editor, Philosophy and Religion

Rosen Educational Services
Alexandra Hanson-Harding: Editor
Shalini Saxena: Editor
Nelson Sá: Art Director
Cindy Reiman: Photography Manager
Matthew Cauli: Designer, Cover Design
Introduction by Brian Duignan

Library of Congress Cataloging-in-Publication Data

Ancient philosophy: from 600 BCE to 500 CE / edited by Brian Duignan.
    p. cm.—(The history of philosophy)
"In association with Britannica Educational Publishing, Rosen Educational Services."
Includes bibliographical references and index.
ISBN 978-1-61530-141-6 (library binding)
1. Philosophy, Ancient. I. Duignan, Brian.
B108.A53 2010
180—dc22

                                                                    2009054263

Manufactured in the United States of America

On the cover: Plato was one of the greatest philosophers ever to have lived. Fuelled by a
desire to fully comprehend the nature of reality, Plato, along with his teacher, Socrates, and
his student, Aristotle, largely pioneered the development of Western philosophical thought.
Today, everything from metaphysics to ethics to political philosophy owes much the work
of Plato and his contemporaries. *Hulton Archive/Getty Images*

On page 16: Thales, shown here, is the first known Greek philosopher and one of the
Seven Wise Men of antiquity. His belief that water formed the basis of the universe marked
a significant deviation from the more widespread myth-based explanations of the time.
Hulton Archive/Getty Images

CONTENTS

Mºore than 2,500 years ago, in the early 6th century BCE, a few inhabitants of the Greek city of Miletus (on the western coast of what is now Turkey) began to think about the world in a new way. Like many people before them, they wondered how the world was created, what it is made of, and why it changes (or seems to change) as it does. Unlike their predecessors, however, the Milesians attempted to answer these questions in natural rather than religious terms. They appealed to what they thought were causes and principles in the world itself, rather than to the acts of gods or other divine beings. Importantly, they believed that the proper way to understand the world is through reason and observation. Because they speculated about profoundly important questions in a rational and systematic way, the Milesians are recognized as the first Western philosophers.

During the 6th century BCE the Greeks also became the first people to practice science and mathematics in the modern sense of those terms. By the middle of the 3rd century BCE the Greeks had produced a finished system of geometrical reasoning (that of Euclid) that would not be significantly amended for more than 2,000 years; by the end of the 4th century they had created nearly all of the basic problems, concepts, methods, and vocabulary of subsequent Western philosophy. Until the late 3rd century CE, other philosophers from the Greek world produced sophisticated and original theories in ethics, epistemology (the study of knowledge), metaphysics (the study of the ultimate nature of reality), and logic. Starting in the first

Plato founded the Academy outside Athens in the 380s BCE where followers of his philosophy were taught in subjects like mathematics, dialectics, and natural science. He is shown here speaking with his students. Museo Archeologico Nazionale, Naples, Italy/The Bridgeman Art Library/ Getty Images

century CE, Jewish and, later, Christian thinkers adopted aspects of the metaphysical system of the Greek philosopher Plato (428–348 BCE) to help them defend and clarify the doctrines of their faiths.

What is called the ancient period in the history of Western philosophy is traditionally divided into four periods, or phases: the Pre-Socratic, extending from the early 6th century to about the mid 4th century BCE; the Classical, to the end of the 2nd century BCE; the Hellenistic, up to the late 1st century BCE; and the Roman, or Imperial, to the early 6th century CE, ending with the fall of the Western Roman Empire.

The term "Pre-Socratic" refers to philosophers who were not influenced by Socrates (470–399 BCE), in most cases because they lived before him. Unfortunately, no work of any Pre-Socratic philosopher has survived; what is known of their teachings consists of various (mostly critical) references in works by later philosophers, especially Plato and Aristotle.

The Milesians, as we have seen, were the first to speculate rationally about the origin and nature of the world; for this reason they and others like them are called "cosmologists." The first of the Milesians, Thales, held that everything is water, by which he meant that the different substances of which the world appears to be composed are ultimately derived from water. The two other members of the "Milesian school," Anaximander (610–546 BCE) and Anaximines (flourished 545 BCE), along with later cosmologists from other Greek cities, proposed various numbers and varieties of primordial substances and various processes by which they were transformed into one another. Anaximander was also noteworthy for advancing a theory of the evolution of living things: humans and all other animals, he said, evolved from fishes. Heraclitus of Ephesus asserted that the basic substance is fire and the basic process "strife"; the apparent unity and permanence of things in the world are the result of the constant conflict of opposites. Thus everything is in a state of flux, or constant change, a view he famously expressed by saying, "You cannot step into the same river twice." Parmenides, who was born in the Greek city of Elea in southern Italy in 515 BCE, argued to the contrary that nothing changes, and the apparent multiplicity of things in the world is an illusion: "all is one." His disciple Zeno of Elea (495–430 BCE) is famous for inventing a series of quite sophisticated paradoxes (apparently valid arguments that lead to absurd conclusions) designed to show that all multiplicity and change are impossible; some of these arguments were not definitively refuted until the 20th century.

The philosopher and mystic Pythagoras (580–500 BCE), traditionally considered the first great mathematician in history, proposed that "all things are numbers," by which he appeared to mean that the structure of each thing and of nature as a whole consists of certain numerical ratios, just as a specific musical harmony is a ratio between the lengths of the physical instruments (e.g., strings or pipes) used to produce it. Pythagoras is known to all students of geometry as the discoverer of the Pythagorean theorem, which states that, in a right triangle, the sum of the squares of the sides is equal to the square of the hypotenuse ($a^2 + b^2 = c^2$). He also made a number of philosophical and religious (or mystical) assertions that would be influential among philosophers of the Classical and Hellenistic periods; for example, he held that the human soul is immortal and is reincarnated into different living things, sometimes human and sometimes animal (it was for this reason that Pythagoras and his followers practiced vegetarianism). The term Pythagoreanism refers both to the doctrines of Pythagoras himself and to the school of thought he founded; the latter, in the form of Neo-Pythagoreanism, was influential in the Hellenistic period of ancient philosophy.

The Pre-Socratic philosophers also included a group of thinkers whose chief concerns were not cosmological but ethical and political. The Sophists, who were active in the 5th century BCE, were itinerant scholars who taught rhetoric and forensics (the art of argument) for money. Because the usual point of their instruction was not knowledge or truth but victory in court, they tended to be dismissive of the notions of certainty, objective truth, and absolute right or wrong. They were utterly despised by Plato, who went to great lengths in some of his dialogues to refute their skepticism and relativism.

The Classical period of ancient philosophy is dominated by three figures of the 5th and 4th centuries BCE, all of them citizens of Athens: Socrates, Plato, and Aristotle. Socrates concerned himself entirely with ethics, what he called the "care of the soul." In part because he was associated with some of the men who conspired to overthrow the democracy in Athens in 404 BCE, he was brought to trial on charges of impiety and corrupting the young and executed in 399 BCE. His refusal to save himself by agreeing to cease his philosophizing made him a model of intellectual and moral integrity for later ages.

Socrates is an enigmatic figure because what is known of his teachings comes almost entirely from the dialogues of his student Plato (Socrates himself wrote nothing). In some of these works a character named Socrates refutes those who pretend to have knowledge of the ethical virtues (e.g., courage), and in others he does this while also putting forth certain ethical, political, and metaphysical doctrines of his own—doctrines that the real, historical Socrates may or may not have held. It is now generally agreed, however, that Plato, not Socrates, is responsible for the theory of ideal properties, or "forms" (such as the

Beautiful and the Hot), which exist separately from the things that have them; for the theory of justice as a harmony between the different parts of the soul; and for the plan, presented in the dialogue Republic, for a utopian city-state ruled by "philosopher-kings."

Plato's greatest student, Aristotle, made foundational contributions to every branch of philosophy, as well as to what would now be called anatomy, biology, physiology, psychology, political science, and poetics. The discipline of logic was his creation. He made important modifications in Plato's theory of forms, holding that forms do not exist apart from the things that have them. His notion of the "final cause" of a thing as the purpose it serves or the goal toward which it strives became the basis of the so-called "teleological" (from Greek *telos*: "end") argument for the existence of God, which has appeared in various forms from late antiquity to the present day. (The contemporary theory of Intelligent Design is a teleological argument.) In ethics Aristotle is known for his subtle and insightful analyses of the virtues and vices and for his theory of human flourishing ("happiness") as the practice of intellectual and moral virtue.

After the death of Alexander the Great, who as king of Macedonia (336–323 BCE) had conquered the entire eastern Mediterranean and the Middle East, his territories were divided by his former generals into hereditary kingdoms. The Greek city-state was long dead, and with it the possibility of meaningful participation in public affairs by ordinary citizens. Philosophy accordingly turned inward, emphasizing the achievement of individual tranquility, contentment, or salvation in a chaotic world.

The philosophical school of Stoicism, founded by Zeno of Citium (335–263 BCE), took to heart Socrates' conviction that the only thing worth having is virtue; all other supposed goods (e.g., health and wealth) are meaningless.

The Stoics also followed Socrates in holding that virtue is a form of knowledge, in the sense that a person who understands the virtues will automatically act virtuously (morally wrong action, in other words, is the result of a misunderstanding about what is actually good or right). The greatest good for the individual is cultivating ethical wisdom and acting in accordance with the divine Reason, or Logos (Greek: "word"), that governs the universe. Stoic philosophy thus enabled its practitioners to achieve repose and tranquility in the face of life's inevitable misfortunes and tragedies. Later forms of Stoicism, which emphasized the ethical duty of public service, exerted a profound influence over many eminent Roman scholars and statesman, including Cicero (106–43 BCE), Seneca (4 BCE–65 CE), and the emperor Marcus Aurelius (121–180 CE).

In contrast to Stoicism, the Epicurean school of philosophy, founded by Epicurus (341–270 BCE), taught that the only good for human beings is pleasure and the only evil pain. Yet it was not a simple hedonism (the pursuit of pleasure for its own sake), because it advocated virtuous action and the avoidance of unattainable desires, which can only bring frustration. Epicureanism promoted a life of quiet retirement and simple but sublime pleasure, the highest form of which is friendship.

During the Hellenistic period the philosophical skepticism of the Sophists and other Pre-Socratics was developed in sophisticated ways by Pyrrhon of Elis (360–272 BCE) and his followers. Although there were many variations, the basic doctrine of Pyrrhonian skepticism was that nothing can be known with certainty because there are always equally good reasons for believing or denying any positive assertion. Pyrrhonian skepticism was a major current in philosophy during the 18th-century Enlightenment, and in one form or another it is still a viable position in contemporary epistemology.

During the Roman period, which began with the fall of the Roman Republic in 31 BCE, philosophy continued to be largely a Greek enterprise—the Romans made no original contributions to philosophy. Stoicism, because of its adoption by members of the Roman elite, was the most influential school of the period, though other Hellenistic schools continued to attract followers. In the 2nd and especially the 3rd centuries CE the philosophy of Plato was revived and transformed through the introduction of various religious and mystical elements, most notably in the Neoplatonism of Plotinus (205–270).

The most significant development of the Roman period, however, was the integration of Christian theology with Neoplatonic philosophy, undertaken by several Christian bishops and other teachers starting in the late 2nd century. The most original and sophisticated of these efforts was that of the 5th-century bishop Saint Augustine. His distinction between the sensible and the intelligible (between what can be known through the senses and what can be known only through the mind), his conception of God and the intelligible realm as existing outside space and time, his understanding of the nature of the soul, his analysis of knowledge, and his treatment of the problem of free will guided philosophical discussion of these topics during the Middle Ages up to about the 13th century, when the philosophy of Aristotle eclipsed that of Plato in medieval universities.

Because it was invented by the ancient Greeks, and because it still reflects ancient Greek influences, Western philosophy is impossible to understand without an appreciation of its ancient history. The figures that you will encounter in this book, some of the greatest geniuses who ever lived, deserve special attention, not only from students of philosophy but also from anyone who wishes to understand the intellectual worldview of the West—how all people in the West see the universe, the divine, and themselves.

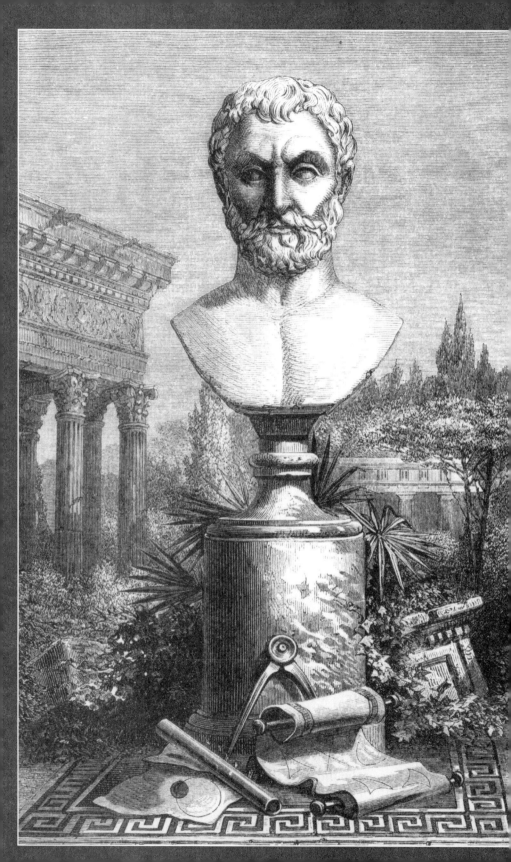

CHAPTER 1

EARLY GREEK PHILOSOPHY: THE PRE-SOCRATICS

Western philosophy emerged in ancient Greece (which included Miletus and other parts of present-day Turkey) in approximately the 6th century BCE. During that time religious awe among the Greeks was eclipsed by wonder about the origin and nature of the physical world. As Greek populations increasingly left the land to become concentrated in city-states, interest shifted from nature to social living. Questions of law and convention and civic values

The map above depicts Greece in the 7th century BCE, prior to the emergence of Western philosophy. The decline of tribal living and the accompanying concentration of Greeks in city-states in the 6th century BCE resulted in the rise of abstract and complex theorizing. Courtesy of the University of Texas Libraries, The University of Texas at Austin

became paramount, and cosmological speculation partly gave way to moral and political theorizing, best exemplified in the somewhat fragmentary ethical philosophies of Socrates (470–399 BCE) and the Sophists (itinerant lecturers and teachers) and in the great positive philosophical systems of Plato (*c.* 428–*c.* 348 BCE) and Aristotle (384–322 BCE). Because they were not influenced by Socrates, the 6th- and 5th-century cosmologists together with the Sophists are often called "pre-Socratic" philosophers, though not all of them lived before Socrates.

COSMOLOGY, METAPHYSICS, AND EPISTEMOLOGY

The first Greek cosmologists were monists, holding that the universe is derived from, or made up of, only a single substance. Later thinkers adopted pluralistic theories, according to which several ultimate substances are involved.

THE EARLY COSMOLOGISTS

There is a consensus, dating back at least to Aristotle and continuing to the present, that the first Greek philosopher was Thales (flourished 6th century BCE). In Thales' time the word *philosopher* ("lover of wisdom") had not yet been coined. Thales was counted, however, among the legendary Seven Wise Men (Sophoi), whose name derives from a term that then designated inventiveness and practical wisdom rather than speculative insight. Thales demonstrated these qualities by trying to give the mathematical knowledge that he derived from the Babylonians a more exact foundation and by using it for the solution of practical problems — such as the determination of the distance of a ship as seen from the shore or of the height of the Egyptian pyramids. Although he was also credited with predicting an eclipse of the Sun, it is likely that he merely gave a natural explanation of one on the basis of Babylonian astronomical knowledge.

Thales is considered the first Greek philosopher because he was the first to give a purely natural explanation of the origin of the world, free from mythological ingredients. He held that everything had come out of water—an explanation based on the discovery of fossil sea animals far inland. His tendency (and that of his immediate successors) to give nonmythological explanations was undoubtedly prompted by the fact that all of them lived on the coast of Anatolia (in present-day Turkey), surrounded by a number of nations whose civilizations were much further advanced than that of the Greeks and whose own mythological explanations varied greatly. It appeared necessary, therefore, to make a fresh start on the basis of what a person could observe and infer by looking at the world as it presented itself. This procedure naturally resulted in a tendency to make sweeping generalizations on the basis of rather restricted, though carefully checked, observations.

Thales' disciple and successor, Anaximander (610–546 BCE), tried to give a more elaborate account of the origin and development of the ordered world (the cosmos). According to him, it developed out of the *apeiron* ("unlimited"), something both infinite and indefinite (without distinguishable qualities). Within this *apeiron*, something arose to produce the opposites of hot and cold. These at once began to struggle with each other and produced the cosmos. The cold (and wet) partly dried up to become solid earth, partly remained as water, and—by means of the hot—partly evaporated, becoming air and mist, its evaporating part (by expansion) splitting up the hot into fiery rings, which surround the whole cosmos. Because these rings are enveloped by mist, however, there remain only certain breathing holes that are visible to human beings, appearing to them as the Sun, the Moon, and the stars.

Anaximander was the first to realize that upward and downward are not absolute but that downward means toward the middle of the Earth and upward away from it, so that the Earth had no need to be supported (as Thales had believed) by anything. Starting from Thales' observations, Anaximander tried to reconstruct the development of life in more detail. Life, being closely bound up with moisture, originated in the sea. All land animals, he held, are descendants of sea animals; because the first humans as newborn infants could not have survived without parents, Anaximander believed that they were born within an animal of another kind—specifically, a sea animal in which

Rendering of Anaximander, one of the first Greek philosophers to develop a cosmology, or theory of the nature and origins of the physical world. Hulton Archive/Getty Images

they were nurtured until they could fend for themselves. Gradually, however, the moisture will be partly evaporated, until in the end all things will return into the undifferentiated *apeiron*, "in order to pay the penalty for their injustice"—that of having struggled against one another.

Anaximander's successor, Anaximenes (flourished mid-6th century BCE), taught that air was the origin of all things. His position was for a long time thought to have been a step backward, because, like Thales, he placed a special kind of matter at the beginning of the development of the world. But this criticism missed the point. Neither Thales nor Anaximander appear to have specified the way in which the other things arose out of water or *apeiron*. Anaximenes, however, declared that the other types of matter arose out of air by condensation and rarefaction. In this way, what to Thales had been merely a beginning became a fundamental principle that remained essentially the same through all of its transmutations. Thus, the term *arche*, which originally simply meant "beginning," acquired the new meaning of "principle," a term that henceforth played an enormous role in philosophy down to the present. This concept of a principle that remains the same through many transmutations is, furthermore, the presupposition of the idea that nothing can come out of nothing and that all of the comings to be and passings away that human beings observe are nothing but transmutations of something that essentially remains the same eternally. In this way it also lies at the bottom of all of the conservation laws—the laws of the conservation of matter, force, and energy—that have been basic in the development of physics. Although Anaximenes of course did not realize all of the implications of his idea, its importance can scarcely be exaggerated.

The first three Greek philosophers have often been called "hylozoists" because they seemed to believe in a kind of living matter. But this is far from an adequate characterization. It is, rather, characteristic of them that they did not clearly distinguish between kinds of matter, forces, and qualities, nor between physical and emotional qualities. The same entity is sometimes called "fire" and sometimes "the hot." Heat appears sometimes as a force and sometimes as a quality, and again there is no clear distinction between warm and cold as physical qualities and the warmth of love and the cold of hate. These ambiguities are important to an understanding of certain later developments in Greek philosophy.

Xenophanes of Colophon (560–478 BCE), a rhapsodist (reciter of poetry) and philosophical thinker who emigrated from Anatolia to the Greek city of Elea in southern Italy, was the first to articulate more clearly what was implied in Anaximenes' philosophy. He criticized the popular notions of the gods, saying that people made the gods in their own image. But, more importantly, he argued that there could be only one God, the ruler of the universe, who must be eternal. For, being the strongest of all beings, he could not have come out of something less strong, nor could he be overcome or superseded by something else, because nothing could arise that is stronger than the strongest. The argument clearly rested on the axioms that nothing can come out of nothing and that nothing that exists can vanish.

These axioms were made more explicit and carried to their logical (and extreme) conclusions by Parmenides of Elea (born c. 515 BCE), the founder of the so-called school of Eleaticism, of whom Xenophanes has been regarded as the teacher and forerunner. In a philosophical poem, Parmenides insisted that "what is" cannot have come into being and cannot pass away because it would have to have come out of nothing or to become nothing, whereas nothing by its very nature does not exist. There can be no motion either, for it would have to be a motion into something that is—which is not possible since it would be blocked—or a motion into something that is not—which is equally impossible since what is not does not exist. Hence, everything is solid, immobile being. The familiar world, in which things move around, come into being, and pass away, is a world of mere belief (*doxa*). In a second part of the poem, however, Parmenides tried to give an analytical account of this world of belief, showing that it rested on constant distinctions between what is believed to be positive—i.e., to have real being, such as light and warmth—and what is believed to be negative—i.e., the absence of positive being, such as darkness and cold.

It is significant that Heracleitus of Ephesus (*c.* 540–*c.* 480 BCE), whose philosophy was later considered to be the very opposite of Parmenides' philosophy of immobile being, came, in some fragments of his work, near to what Parmenides tried to show: the positive and the negative, he said, are merely different views of the same thing; death and life, day and night, and light and darkness are really one.

Viewing fire as the essential material uniting all things, Heracleitus wrote that the world order is an "ever-living fire kindling in measures and being extinguished in measures." He extended the manifestations of fire to include not only fuel, flame, and smoke but also the ether in the upper atmosphere. Part of this air, or pure fire, "turns to" ocean, presumably as rain, and part of the ocean turns to earth. Simultaneously, equal masses of earth and sea everywhere are returning to the respective aspects of sea and fire. The resulting dynamic equilibrium maintains an orderly balance in the world. This persistence of unity despite change is illustrated by Heracleitus' famous analogy of life to a river: "Upon those who step into the same rivers different and ever different waters flow down." Plato later took this doctrine to mean that all things are in constant flux, regardless of how they appear to the senses.

Being and Becoming

Parmenides had an enormous influence on the further development of philosophy. Most of the philosophers of the following two generations tried to find a way to reconcile his thesis that nothing comes into being nor passes away with the evidence presented to the senses. Empedocles of Acragas (c. 490–430 BCE) declared that there are four material elements (he called them the roots of everything) and two forces, love and hate, that did not come into being and would never pass away, increase, or diminish. But the elements are constantly mixed with one another by love and again separated by hate. Thus, through mixture and decomposition, composite things come into being and pass away. Because Empedocles conceived of love and hate as blind forces, he had to explain how, through random motion, living beings could emerge. This he did by means of a somewhat crude anticipation of the theory of the survival of the fittest. In the process of mixture and decomposition, the limbs and parts of various animals would be formed by chance. But they could not survive on their own; they would survive only when, by chance, they had come together in such a way that they were able to support and reproduce themselves. It was in this way that the various species were produced and continued to exist.

Anaxagoras of Clazomenae (c. 500–c. 428 BCE), a pluralist, believed that because nothing can really come into being, everything must be contained in everything, but in the form of infinitely small parts. In the beginning, all of these particles had existed in an even mixture, in which nothing could be distinguished, much like the indefinite *apeiron* of Anaximander. But then nous, or intelligence, began at one point to set these particles into a whirling motion, foreseeing that in this way they would become separated from one another and then recombine in the most various ways so as to produce gradually the world in which human beings live. In contrast to the forces assumed by Empedocles, the nous of Anaxagoras is not blind but foresees and intends the production of the cosmos, including living and intelligent beings; however, it does not interfere with the process after having started the whirling motion. This is a strange combination of a mechanical and a nonmechanical explanation of the world.

By far of greatest importance for the later development of philosophy and physical science was an attempt by Leucippus (flourished 5th century BCE) and Democritus (*c.* 460–*c.* 370 BCE) to solve the Parmenidean problem. Leucippus found the solution in the assumption that, contrary to Parmenides' argument, the nothing does in a way exist—as empty space. There are, then, two fundamental principles of the physical world, empty space and filled space—the latter consisting of atoms that, in contrast to those of modern physics, are real atoms—that is, they are absolutely indivisible because nothing can penetrate to split them. On these foundations, laid by Leucippus, Democritus appears to have built a whole system, aiming at a complete explanation of the varied phenomena of the visible world by means of an analysis of its atomic structure. This system begins with elementary physical problems, such as why a hard body can be lighter than a softer one. The explanation is that the heavier body contains more atoms, which are equally distributed and of round shape; the lighter body, however, has fewer atoms, most of which have hooks by which they form rigid gratings. The system ends with educational and ethical questions. A sound and cheerful person, useful to his fellows, is literally well composed. Although destructive passions involve violent, long-distance atomic motions, education can help to contain them, creating a better composure. Democritus also developed a theory of the evolution of culture, which influenced later thinkers. Civilization, he thought, is produced by the needs of life, which compel human beings to work and to make inventions. When life becomes too easy because all needs are met, there is a danger that civilization will decay as people become unruly and negligent.

APPEARANCE AND REALITY

All of the post-Parmenidean philosophers, like Parmenides himself, presupposed that the real world is different from the one that human beings perceive. Thus arose the problems of epistemology, or theory of knowledge. According to Anaxagoras, everything is contained in everything. But this is not what people perceive. He solved this problem by postulating that, if there is a much greater amount of one kind of particle in a thing than of all other kinds, the latter are not perceived at all. The observation was then made that sometimes different persons or kinds of animals have different perceptions of the same things. He explained this phenomenon by assuming that like is perceived by like. If, therefore, in the sense organ of one person there is less of one kind of stuff than of another, that person will perceive the former less keenly than the latter. This reasoning was also used to explain why some animals see better at night and others during the day.

According to Democritus, atoms have no sensible qualities, such as taste, smell, or colour, at all. Thus, he tried to reduce all of them to tactile qualities (explaining a bright white colour, for instance, as sharp atoms hitting the eye like needles), and he made a most elaborate attempt to reconstruct the atomic structure of things on the basis of their apparent sensible qualities.

Also of very great importance in the history of epistemology was Zeno of Elea (c. 495–c. 430 BCE), a younger friend of Parmenides. Parmenides had, of course, been severely criticized because of the strange consequences of his doctrine: that in reality there is no motion and no plurality because there is just one solid being. To support him, however, Zeno tried to show that the assumption that there is motion and plurality leads to consequences that are no less strange. This he did by means of his famous paradoxes, saying that the flying arrow rests since it can neither move in the place in which it is nor in a place in which it is not, and that Achilles cannot outrun a turtle because, when he has reached its starting point, the turtle will have moved to a further point, and so on ad infinitum—that, in fact, he cannot even start running, for, before traversing the stretch to the starting point of the turtle, he will have to traverse half of it, and again half of that, and so on ad infinitum. All of these paradoxes are derived from what is known as the problem of the continuum. Although they have often been dismissed as logical nonsense, many attempts have also been made to dispose of them by means of mathematical theorems, such as the theory of convergent series or the theory of sets. In the end, however, the logical difficulties raised in Zeno's arguments have always come back with a vengeance, for the human mind is so constructed that it can look at a continuum in two ways that are not quite reconcilable.

Pythagoras and Pythagoreanism

All of the philosophies mentioned so far are in various ways historically akin to one another. Toward the end of the 6th century BCE, however, there arose, quite independently, another kind of philosophy, which only later entered into interrelation with the developments just mentioned: the philosophy of Pythagoras of Samos (*c.* 580–*c.* 500 BCE). Pythagoras traveled extensively in the Middle East and in Egypt and, after his return to Samos (an island off the coast of Anatolia), emigrated to southern Italy because of his dislike of the tyranny of Polycrates (*c.* 535–522 BCE). At Croton and Metapontum he founded a philosophical society with strict rules and soon gained considerable political influence. He appears to have brought his doctrine of the transmigration (reincarnation) of souls from the Middle East. Much more important for the history of philosophy and science, however, was his doctrine that "all things are numbers," which means that the essence and structure of all things can be determined by finding the numerical relations they express. Originally, this, too, was a very broad generalization made on the basis of comparatively few observations: for instance, that the same harmonies can be produced with different instruments—strings, pipes, disks, etc.—by means of the same numerical ratios—1:2, 2:3, 3:4—in one-dimensional extensions; the observation that certain regularities exist in the movements of the celestial bodies; and the discovery that the form of a triangle is determined by the ratio of the lengths of its sides. But because the followers of Pythagoras tried to apply their principle everywhere with the greatest of accuracy, one of them—Hippasus of Metapontum (flourished 5th century BCE)—made one of the most fundamental discoveries in the entire history of science: that the side and diagonal of simple figures such as the square and the regular pentagon are incommensurable—i.e., their quantitative relation cannot be expressed as a ratio of integers. At first sight this discovery seemed to destroy the very basis of the Pythagorean philosophy, and the school thus split into two sects, one of which engaged in rather abstruse numerical speculations, while the other succeeded in overcoming the difficulty by ingenious mathematical inventions. Pythagorean philosophy also exerted a great influence on the later development of Plato's thought.

The speculations described so far constitute, in many ways, the most important part of the history of Greek philosophy because all of the most fundamental problems of Western philosophy turned up here for the first time. One also finds here the formation of a great many concepts that have continued to dominate Western philosophy and science to the present day.

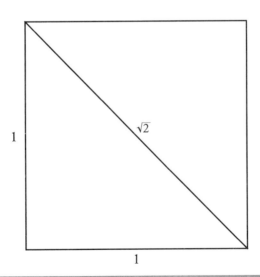

Hippasus, a follower of Pythagoras, was the first to realize that not all quantities can be expressed as a whole number or the ratio of two whole numbers (a fraction). For example, a simple square with sides equal to 1 unit each would have a diagonal equal to $\sqrt{2}$, an irrational number.

SKEPTICISM AND RELATIVISM: THE SOPHISTS

In the middle of the 5th century BCE, Greek thinking took a somewhat different turn through the advent of the Sophists. The name is derived from the verb *sophizesthai*, "making a profession of being inventive and clever," and aptly described the Sophists, who, in contrast to the philosophers mentioned so far, charged fees for their instruction.

Philosophically, the Sophists were, in a way, the leaders of a rebellion against the preceding development of philosophy, which increasingly had resulted in the belief that the real world is quite different from the phenomenal world. "What is the sense of such speculations?" they asked, since no one lives in these so-called real worlds. This is the meaning of the pronouncement of Protagoras of Abdera (*c.* 485–*c.* 410 BCE) that "man is the measure of all things, of those which are that they are and of those which are not that they are not." For human beings the world is what it appears to them to be, not something else; Protagoras illustrated his point by saying that it makes no sense to tell a person that it is really warm when he is shivering with cold because for him it is cold—for him, the cold exists, is there.

His younger contemporary Gorgias of Leontini (flourished 5th century BCE), famous for his treatise on the art of oratory, made fun of the philosophers in his book *Peri tou mē ontos ē peri physeōs* ("On That Which Is Not; or, On Nature"), in which—referring to the "truly existing world," also called "the nature of things"—he tried to prove (1) that nothing exists, (2) that if something existed, one could have no knowledge of it, and (3) that if nevertheless somebody knew something existed, he could not communicate his knowledge to others.

The Sophists were not only skeptical of what had by then become a philosophical tradition but also of other traditions. On the basis of the observation that different nations have different rules of conduct even in regard to things considered most sacred—such as the relations between the sexes, marriage, and burial—they concluded that most rules of conduct are conventions. What is really important is to be successful in life and to gain influence over others. This they promised to teach. Gorgias was proud of the fact that, having no knowledge of medicine, he was more successful in persuading a patient to undergo a necessary operation than his brother, a physician, who knew when an operation was necessary. The older Sophists, however, were far from openly preaching immoralism. They, nevertheless, gradually came under suspicion because of their sly ways of arguing. One of the later Sophists, Thrasymachus of Chalcedon (flourished 5th century BCE), was bold enough to declare openly that "right is what is beneficial for the stronger or better one"—that is, for the one able to win the power to bend others to his will.

CHAPTER 2

THE PHILOSOPHY
OF SOCRATES

The life, character, and thought of Socrates (*c.* 470–399 BCE) have exerted a profound influence on Western philosophy from ancient times to the present day.

Socrates was a widely recognized and controversial figure in his native Athens, so much so that he was frequently mocked in the plays of comic dramatists. (The *Clouds* of Aristophanes, produced in 423, is the best-known example.) Although Socrates himself wrote nothing, he is depicted in conversation in compositions by a small circle of his admirers—Plato and Xenophon first among them. He is portrayed in these works as a man of great insight, integrity, self-mastery, and argumentative skill. The impact of his life was all the greater because of the way in which it ended: at age 70, he was brought to trial on a charge of impiety and sentenced to death by poisoning (the poison probably being hemlock) by a jury of his fellow citizens. Plato's *Apology of Socrates* purports to be the speech Socrates gave at his trial in response to the accusations made against him (the Greek term *apologia* means "defense"). Its powerful advocacy of the examined life and its condemnation of Athenian democracy have made it one of the central documents of Western thought and culture.

HIS LIFE AND PERSONALITY

Although literary and philosophical sources provide only a small amount of information about the life and personality of Socrates, a unique and vivid picture is available to us in the works of Plato. We know the names of his father, Sophroniscus (probably a stonemason), his mother, Phaenarete, and his wife, Xanthippe, and we know that he had three sons. With a snub nose and bulging eyes, which made him always appear to be

Socrates, herm with a restored nose probably copied from the Greek original by Lysippus, c. 350 BCE. In the Museo Archeologico Nazionale, Naples. Courtesy of the Soprintendenza alle Antichita della Campania, Naples

staring, he was unattractive by conventional standards. He served as a hoplite (a heavily armed soldier) in the Athenian army and fought bravely in several important battles. Unlike many of the thinkers of his time, he did not travel to other cities in order to pursue his intellectual interests. Although he did not seek high office, did not regularly attend meetings of the Athenian Assembly (Ecclesia), the city's principal governing body (as was his privilege as an adult male citizen), and was not active in any political faction, he discharged his duties as a citizen, which included not only military service but occasional membership in the Council of Five Hundred, which prepared the Assembly's agenda.

The Pnyx is a hill west of the Acropolis where the Ecclesia, or Assembly, the centre of the Athenian government, convened regularly. Though Socrates did not actively participate in politics, he held strong views on democracy and the proceedings of the Assembly. Dmitri Kessel/Time & Life Pictures/ Getty Images

Socrates was not well-born or wealthy, but many of his admirers were, and they included several of the most politically prominent Athenian citizens. When the democratic constitution of Athens was overthrown for a brief time in 403, four years before his trial, he did not leave the city, as did many devoted supporters of democratic rule, including his friend Chaerephon, who had gone to Delphi many years earlier to ask the oracle whether anyone was wiser than Socrates. (The answer was no.) Socrates' long fits of abstraction, his courage in battle, his resistance to hunger and cold, his ability to consume wine without apparent inebriation, and his extraordinary self-control in the presence of sensual attractions are all described with consummate artistry in the opening and closing pages of the *Symposium*.

Socrates' personality was in some ways closely connected to his philosophical outlook. He was remarkable for the absolute command he maintained over his emotions and his apparent indifference to physical hardships. Corresponding to these personal qualities was his commitment to the doctrine that reason, properly cultivated, can and ought to be the all-controlling factor in human life. Thus he has no fear of death, he says in Plato's *Apology*, because he has no knowledge of what comes after it, and he holds that, if anyone does fear death, his fear can be based only on a pretense of knowledge. The assumption underlying this claim is that, once one has given sufficient thought to some matter, one's emotions will follow suit. Fear will be dispelled by intellectual clarity. Similarly, according to Socrates, if one believes, upon reflection, that one should act in a particular way, then, necessarily, one's feelings about the act in question will accommodate themselves to one's belief—one will desire to act in that way. (Thus, Socrates denies the possibility of what has been called "weakness of will"—knowingly acting in a way one believes to be wrong.) It follows that, once one knows what virtue is, it is impossible not to act virtuously. Anyone who fails to act virtuously does so because he incorrectly identifies virtue with something it is not. This is what is meant by the thesis, attributed to Socrates by Aristotle, that virtue is a form of knowledge.

Socrates' conception of virtue as a form of knowledge explains why he takes it to be of the greatest importance to seek answers to questions such as "What is courage?" and "What is piety?" If we could just discover the answers to these questions, we would have all we need to live our lives well. The fact that Socrates achieved a complete rational control of his emotions no doubt encouraged him to suppose that his own case was indicative of what human beings at their best can achieve.

But if virtue is a form of knowledge, does that mean that each of the virtues—courage, piety, justice—constitutes a separate branch of knowledge, and should we infer that it is possible to acquire knowledge of one of these branches but not of the others? This is an issue that emerges in several of Plato's dialogues; it is most fully discussed in *Protagoras*. It was a piece of conventional Greek wisdom, and is still widely assumed, that one can have some admirable qualities but lack others. One might, for example, be courageous but unjust. Socrates challenges this assumption; he believes that the many virtues form a kind of unity—though, not being able to define any of the virtues, he is in no position to say whether they are all the same thing or instead constitute some looser kind of unification. But he unequivocally rejects the conventional idea that one can possess one virtue without possessing them all.

Another prominent feature of the personality of Socrates, one that often creates problems about how best to interpret him, is (to use the ancient Greek term) his *eirôneia*. Although this is the term from which the English word *irony* is derived, there is a difference between the two. To speak ironically is to use words to mean the opposite of what they normally convey, but it is not necessarily to aim at deception, for the speaker may expect and even want the audience to recognize this reversal. In contrast, for the ancient Greeks *eirôneia* meant "dissembling"—a user of *eirôneia* is trying to hide something. This is the accusation that is made against Socrates several times in Plato's works (though never in Xenophon's). Socrates says in Plato's *Apology*, for example, that the jurors hearing his case will not accept the reason he offers for being unable to stop his philosophizing in the marketplace—that to do so would be to disobey the god who presides at Delphi (Socrates' audience understood him to be referring to Apollo, though he does not himself use this name. Throughout his speech, he affirms his obedience to the god or to the gods but not specifically to one or more of the familiar gods or goddesses of the Greek pantheon). The cause of their incredulity, he adds, will be their assumption that he is engaging in *eirôneia*. In effect, Socrates is admitting that he has acquired a reputation for insincerity—for giving people to understand that his words mean what they are ordinarily taken to mean when in fact they do not. Similarly, in Book I of the *Republic*, Socrates is accused by a hostile interlocutor, Thrasymachus, of "habitual *eirôneia*." Although Socrates says that he does

The Greek god Apollo, whose temple in Delphi is shown above, earned the devotion of Socrates. Apollo's oracle at Delphi stated that there was no one wiser than Socrates. Manuel Cohen/Getty Images

not have a good answer to the question "What is justice?," Thrasymachus thinks that this is just a pose. Socrates, he alleges, is concealing his favoured answer. And in the *Symposium*, Alcibiades accuses Socrates of "spending his whole life engaged in *eirôneia* and playing with people" and compares him to a carved figurine whose outer shell conceals its inner contents. The heart of Alcibiades' accusation is that Socrates pretends to care about people and to offer them advantages but withholds what he knows because he is full of disdain.

Plato's portrayal of Socrates as an "ironist" shows how conversation with him could easily lead to a frustrating impasse and how the possibility of resentment was ever present. Socrates was in this sense a masked interlocutor—an aspect of his self-presentation that made him more fascinating and alluring to his audiences but that also added to their distrust and suspicion. And readers, who come to know Socrates through the intervention of Plato, are in somewhat the same situation. Our efforts to interpret him are sometimes not as sound as we would like, because we must rely on judgments, often difficult to justify, about when he means what he says and when he does not.

Even when Socrates goes to court to defend himself against the most serious of charges, he seems to be engaged in *eirôneia*. After listening to the speeches given by his accusers, he says, in the opening sentence of Plato's *Apology*: "I was almost carried away in spite of myself, so persuasively did they speak." Is this the habitual *eirôneia* of Socrates? Or did the speeches of his accusers really have this effect on him? It is difficult to be sure. But, by Socrates' own admission, the suspicion that anything he says might be a pose undermines his ability to persuade the jurors of his good intentions. His *eirôneia* may even have lent support to one of the accusations made against him, that he corrupted the young. For if Socrates really did engage in *eirôneia*, and if his youthful followers delighted in and imitated this aspect of his character, then to that extent he encouraged them to become dissembling and untrustworthy, just like himself.

WHY WAS SOCRATES HATED?

Part of the fascination of Plato's *Apology* consists in the fact that it presents a man who takes extraordinary steps throughout his life to be of the greatest possible value to his community but whose efforts, far from earning him the gratitude and honour he thinks he deserves, lead to his condemnation and death at the hands of the very people he seeks to serve. Socrates is painfully aware that he is a hated figure and that this is what has led to the accusations against him. He has little money and no political savvy or influence, and he has paid little attention to his family and household—all in order to serve the public that now reviles him. What went wrong?

THE IMPRESSION CREATED BY ARISTOPHANES

Socrates goes to some length to answer this question. Much of his defense consists not merely in refuting the charges but in offering a complex explanation of why such false accusations should have been brought against him in the first place. Part of the explanation, he believes, is that he has long been misunderstood by the general public. The public, he says, has focused its distrust of certain types of people upon him. He claims that the false impressions of his "first accusers" (as he calls them) derive from a play of Aristophanes (he is referring to *Clouds*) in which a character called Socrates is seen "swinging about, saying he was walking on air and talking a lot of nonsense about things of which I know nothing at all." The Socrates of Aristophanes' comedy is the head of a school that investigates every sort of empirical phenomenon, regards clouds and air as divine substances, denies the existence of any gods but these, studies language and the art of argument, and uses its knowledge of rhetorical devices to "make the worse into the stronger argument," as the Socrates of the *Apology* puts it in his speech. Socrates' corruption of the young is also a major theme of *Clouds*: it features a father (Strepsiades) who attends Socrates' school with his son (Pheidippides) in order to learn how to avoid paying the debts he has incurred because of his son's extravagance. In the end, Pheidippides learns all too well how to use argumentative skills to his advantage; indeed, he prides himself on his ability to prove that it is right for a son to beat his parents. In the end, Strepsiades denounces Socrates and burns down the building that houses his school.

Amphitheatres, like this one in Syracuse, Sicily, often provided the setting for performances of Aristophanes' Clouds *and other plays.* Fox Photos/Hulton Archive/Getty Images

This play, Socrates says, has created the general impression that he studies celestial and geographic phenomena and, like the Sophists who travel from city to city, takes a fee for teaching the young various skills. Not so, says Socrates. He thinks it would be a fine thing to possess the kinds of knowledge these Sophists claim to teach, but he has never discussed these matters with anyone—as his judges should be able to confirm for themselves, because, he says, many of them have heard his conversations.

THE HUMAN RESISTANCE TO SELF-REFLECTION

But this can only be the beginning of Socrates' explanation, for it leads to further questions. Why should Aristophanes have written in this way about Socrates? The latter must have been a well-known figure in 423, when *Clouds* was produced, for Aristophanes typically wrote about and mocked figures who already were familiar to his audience. Furthermore, if, as Socrates claims, many of his jurors had heard him in discussion and could therefore confirm for themselves that he did not study or teach others about clouds, air, and other such matters and did not take a fee as the Sophists did, then why did they not vote to acquit him of the charges by an overwhelming majority?

Socrates provides answers to these questions. Long before Aristophanes wrote about him, he had acquired a reputation among his fellow citizens because he spent his days attempting to fulfill his divine mission to cross-examine them and to puncture their confident belief that they possessed knowledge of the most important matters. Socrates tells the jurors that, as a result of his inquiries, he has learned a bitter lesson about his fellow citizens: not only do they fail to possess the knowledge they claim to have, but they resent having this fact pointed out to them, and they hate him for his insistence that his reflective way of life and his disavowal of knowledge make him superior to them. The only people who delight in his conversation are the young and wealthy, who have the leisure to spend their days with him. These people imitate him by carrying out their own cross-examinations of their elders. Socrates does admit, then, that he has, to some degree, set one generation against another—and in making this confession, he makes it apparent why some members of the jury may have been convinced, on the basis of their own acquaintance with him, that he has corrupted the city's young.

One of the most subtle components of Socrates' explanation for the hatred he has aroused is his point that people hide the shame they feel when they are unable to withstand his destructive arguments. His reputation as a corrupter of the young and as a Sophist and an atheist is sustained because it provides people with an ostensibly reasonable explanation of their hatred of him. No one will say, "I hate Socrates because I cannot answer his questions, and he makes me look foolish in front of the young." Instead, people hide their shame and the real source of

This bas-relief depicts Socrates (second from the right) *conversing with other men.* Time & Life Pictures/Getty Images

their anger by seizing on the general impression that he is the sort of philosopher who casts doubt on traditional religion and teaches people rhetorical tricks that can be used to make bad arguments look good. These ways of hiding the source of their hatred are all the more potent because they contain at least a grain of truth. Socrates, as both Plato and Xenophon confirm, is a man who loves to argue: in that respect he is like a Sophist. And his conception of piety, as revealed by his devotion to the Delphic oracle, is highly unorthodox: in that respect he is like those who deny the existence of the gods.

Socrates believes that this hatred, whose real source is so painful for people to acknowledge, played a crucial role in leading Meletus, Anytus, and Lycon to come forward in court against him; it also makes it so difficult for many members of the jury to acknowledge that he has the highest motives and has done his city a great service. Aristophanes' mockery of Socrates and the legal indictment against him could not possibly have led to his trial or conviction were it not for something in a large number of his fellow Athenians that wanted to be rid of him. This is a theme to which Socrates returns several times. He compares himself, at one point, to a gadfly who has been assigned by the god to stir a large and sluggish horse. Note what this implies: the bite of the fly cannot be anything but painful, and it is only natural that the horse would like nothing better than to kill it. After the jury has voted in favour of the death penalty, Socrates tells them that their motive has been their desire to avoid giving a defense of their lives. Something in people resists self-examination: they do not want to answer deep questions about themselves, and they hate those who cajole them for not doing so or for doing so poorly. At bottom, Socrates thinks that all but a few people will strike out against those who try to stimulate serious moral reflection in them. That is why he thinks that his trial is not merely the result of unfortuitous events—a mere misunderstanding caused by the work of a popular playwright—but the outcome of psychological forces deep within human nature.

SOCRATES' CRITICISM OF DEMOCRACY

Socrates' analysis of the hatred he has incurred is one part of a larger theme that he dwells on throughout his speech. Athens is a democracy, a city in which the many are the dominant power in politics, and it can therefore be expected to have all the vices of the many. Because most people hate to be tested in argument, they will always take action of some sort against those who provoke them with questions. But that is not the only accusation Socrates brings forward against his city and its politics. He tells his democratic audience that he was right to have withdrawn from political life, because a good person who fights for justice in a democracy will be killed. In his cross-examination of Meletus, he insists that only a few people can acquire the knowledge necessary for improving the young of any species, and that the many will inevitably do a poor job. He criticizes the Assembly for its illegal actions and the Athenian courts for the ease with which matters of justice are distorted by emotional pleading. Socrates implies that the very nature of democracy makes it a corrupt political system. Bitter experience has taught him that most people rest content with a superficial understanding of the most urgent human questions. When they are given great power, their shallowness inevitably leads to injustice.

THE LEGACY OF SOCRATES

Socrates' thought was so pregnant with possibilities, his mode of life so provocative, that he inspired a remarkable variety of responses. One of his associates, Aristippus of Cyrene—his followers were called "Cyrenaics," and their school flourished for a century and a half—affirmed that pleasure is the highest good. (Socrates seems to endorse this thesis in Plato's *Protagoras*, but he attacks it in *Gorgias* and other dialogues.) Another prominent follower of Socrates in the early 4th century BCE, Antisthenes, emphasized the Socratic doctrine that a good man cannot be harmed; virtue, in other words, is by itself sufficient for happiness. That doctrine played a central role in a school of thought, founded by Diogenes of Sinope, that had an enduring influence on Greek and Roman philosophy: Cynicism.

Like Socrates, Diogenes was concerned solely with ethics, practiced his philosophy in the marketplace, and upheld an ideal of indifference to material possessions, political power, and conventional honours. But the Cynics, unlike Socrates, treated all conventional distinctions and cultural traditions as impediments to the life of virtue. They advocated a life in accordance with nature and regarded animals and human beings who did not live in societies as being closer to nature than contemporary human beings. (The term *cynic* is derived from the Greek word for dog. Cynics, therefore, live like beasts.) Starting from the Socratic premise that virtue is sufficient for happiness, they launched attacks on marriage, the family, national distinctions, authority, and cultural achievements. But the two most important ancient schools of thought that were influenced by Socrates were Stoicism, founded by Zeno of Citium, and skepticism which became, for many centuries, the reigning philosophical stance of Plato's Academy after Arcesilaus became its leader in 273 BCE. The influence of Socrates on Zeno was mediated by the Cynics, but Roman Stoics—particularly Epictetus—regarded Socrates as the paradigm of sagacious inner

Diogenes of Sinope, founder of the Cynic school of thought, is depicted above with his fabled lantern. It has been said that he would walk with a lit lantern in broad daylight as part of his quest to find an honest man. Hulton Archive/ Getty Images

strength, and they invented new arguments for the Socratic thesis that virtue is sufficient for happiness. The Stoic doctrine that divine intelligence pervades the world and rules for the best borrows heavily from ideas attributed to Socrates by Xenophon in the *Memorabilia*.

Like Socrates, Arcesilaus wrote nothing. He philosophized by inviting others to state a thesis; he would then prove, by Socratic questioning, that their thesis led to a contradiction. His use of the Socratic method allowed Arcesilaus and his successors in the Academy to hold that they were remaining true to the central theme of Plato's writings. But, just as Cynicism took Socratic themes in a direction Socrates himself had not developed and indeed would have rejected, so, too, Arcesilaus and his skeptical followers in Plato's Academy used the Socratic method to advocate a general suspension of all convictions whatsoever and not merely a disavowal of knowledge. The underlying thought of the Academy during its skeptical phase is that, because there is no way to distinguish truth from falsity, we must refrain from believing anything at all. Socrates, by contrast, merely claims to have no knowledge, and he regards certain theses as far more worthy of our credence than their denials.

Although Socrates exerted a profound influence on Greek and Roman thought, not every major philosopher of antiquity regarded him as a moral exemplar or a major thinker. Aristotle approves of the Socratic search for definitions but criticizes Socrates for an overintellectualized conception of the human psyche. The followers of Epicurus, who were philosophical rivals of the Stoics and Academics, were contemptuous of him.

With the ascendancy of Christianity in the medieval period, the influence of Socrates was at its nadir: he was, for many centuries, little more than an Athenian who had been condemned to death. But when Greek texts, and thus the works of Plato, the Stoics, and the skeptics, became increasingly available in the Renaissance, the thought and personality of Socrates began to play an important role in European philosophy. From the 16th to the 19th century the instability and excesses of Athenian democracy became a common motif of political writers; the hostility of Xenophon and Plato, fed by the death of Socrates, played an important role here. Comparisons between Socrates and Christ became commonplace, and they remained so even into the 20th century—though the contrasts drawn between them, and the uses to which their similarities were put, varied greatly from one author and period to another. The divine sign of Socrates became a matter of controversy: was he truly inspired by the voice of God? Or was the sign only an intuitive and natural grasp of virtue? (So thought Montaigne.) Did he intend to undermine the irrational and merely conventional aspects of religious practice and thus to place religion on a scientific footing? (So thought the 18th-century Deists.)

In the 19th century Socrates was regarded as a seminal figure in the evolution of European thought or as a Christlike herald of a higher existence. G.W.F. Hegel saw in Socrates a decisive turn from pre-reflective moral habits to a self-consciousness that, tragically, had not yet learned how to reconcile itself to universal civic standards. Søren Kierkegaard, whose dissertation examined Socratic irony, found in Socrates a pagan anticipation of his belief that Christianity is a lived doctrine of almost impossible demands; but he also regarded Socratic irony as a deeply flawed indifference to morality. Friedrich Nietzsche struggled throughout his writings against the one-sided rationalism and the destruction of cultural forms that he found in Socrates.

Despite the controversies surrounding his philosophy, Socrates maintained a loyal following and was hailed as a martyr by later philosophers. A copy of Jacques-Louis David's 18th century painting The Death of Socrates *(above) depicts Socrates surrounded by a number of followers before his death by poison.* Hulton Archive/Getty Images

In contrast, in Victorian England Socrates was idealized by utilitarian thinkers as a Christ-like martyr who laid the foundations of a modern, rational, scientific worldview. John Stuart Mill mentions the legal executions of Socrates and of Christ in the same breath in order to call attention to the terrible consequences of allowing common opinion to persecute unorthodox thinkers. Benjamin Jowett, the principal translator of Plato in the late 19th century, told his students at Oxford, "The two biographies about which we are most deeply interested (though not to the same degree) are those of Christ and Socrates." Such comparisons continued into the 20th century: Socrates is treated as a "paradigmatic individual" (along with Buddha, Confucius, and Christ) by the German existentialist philosopher Karl Jaspers.

The conflict between Socrates and Athenian democracy shaped the thought of 20th-century political philosophers such as Leo Strauss, Hannah Arendt, and Karl Popper. The tradition of self-reflection and care of the self-initiated by Socrates fascinated the French philosopher Michel Foucault in his later writings. Analytic philosophy, an intellectual tradition that traces its origins to the work of Gottlob Frege, G.E. Moore, and Bertrand Russell in the late 19th and early 20th century, uses, as one of its fundamental tools, a process called "conceptual analysis," a form of nonempirical inquiry that bears some resemblance to Socrates' search for definitions.

But the influence of Socrates is felt not only among philosophers and others inside the academy. He remains, for all of us, a challenge to complacency and a model of integrity.

CHAPTER 3

THE PHILOSOPHY OF PLATO

Plato, together with his teacher Socrates and his student Aristotle, laid the philosophical foundations of Western culture.

Building on the demonstration by Socrates that those regarded as experts in ethical matters did not have the understanding necessary for a good human life, Plato introduced the idea that their mistakes were due to their not engaging properly with a class of entities he called forms, chief examples of which were Justice, Beauty, and Equality. Whereas other thinkers—and Plato himself in certain passages—used the term without any precise technical force, Plato in the course of his career came to devote specialized attention to these entities. As he conceived them, they were accessible not to the senses but to the mind alone, and they were the most important constituents of reality, underlying the existence of the sensible world and giving it what intelligibility it has. In metaphysics Plato envisioned a systematic, rational treatment of the forms and their interrelations, starting with the most fundamental among them (the Good, or the One); in ethics and moral psychology he developed the view that the good life requires not just a certain kind of knowledge (as Socrates had suggested) but also habituation to healthy emotional responses and therefore harmony between the three parts of the soul (according

to Plato, reason, spirit, and appetite). His works also contain discussions in aesthetics, political philosophy, theology, cosmology, epistemology, and the philosophy of language. His school fostered research not just in philosophy narrowly conceived but in a wide range of endeavours that today would be called mathematical or scientific.

Plato, Roman herm probably copied from a Greek original, 4th century BCE; in the Staatliche Museen, Berlin. Courtesy of the Staatliche Museen zu Berlin

HIS LIFE

The son of Ariston (his father) and Perictione (his mother), Plato was born in 428 BCE, the year after the death of the great Athenian statesman Pericles, and died in 348 BCE. His brothers Glaucon and Adeimantus are portrayed as interlocutors in Plato's masterpiece the *Republic*, and his half brother Antiphon figures in the *Parmenides*. Plato's family was aristocratic and distinguished: his father's side claimed descent from the god Poseidon, and his mother's side was related to the lawgiver Solon (*c.* 630–560 BCE). Less creditably, his mother's close relatives Critias and Charmides were among the Thirty Tyrants who seized power in Athens and ruled briefly until the restoration of democracy in 403.

Plato as a young man was a member of the circle around Socrates. Since the latter wrote nothing, what is known of his characteristic activity of engaging his fellow citizens (and the occasional itinerant celebrity) in conversation derives wholly from the writings of others, most notably Plato himself. The works of Plato commonly referred to as "Socratic" represent the sort of thing the historical Socrates was doing. He would challenge men who supposedly had expertise about some facet of human excellence to give accounts of these matters—variously of courage, piety, and so on, or at times of the whole of "virtue"—and they typically failed to maintain their position. Plato was profoundly affected by both the life and the death of Socrates. The activity of the older man provided the starting point of Plato's philosophizing. Moreover, if Plato's *Seventh Letter* is to be believed (its authorship is disputed), the treatment of Socrates by both the oligarchy and the democracy made Plato wary of entering public life, as someone of his background would normally have done.

After the death of Socrates, Plato may have traveled extensively in Greece, Italy, and Egypt, though on such particulars the evidence is uncertain. The followers of Pythagoras (*c.* 580–*c.* 500 BCE) seem to have influenced his philosophical program (they are criticized in the *Phaedo* and the *Republic* but receive respectful mention in the *Philebus*). It is thought that his three trips to Syracuse in Sicily (many of the *Letters* concern these, though their authenticity is controversial) led to a deep personal attachment to Dion (408–354 BCE), brother-in-law of Dionysius the Elder (430–367 BCE), the tyrant of Syracuse. Plato, at Dion's urging, apparently undertook to put into practice the ideal of the "philosopher-king" (described in the *Republic*) by educating Dionysius the Younger; the project was not a success, and in the ensuing instability Dion was murdered.

Plato's Academy, founded in the 380s and located on the outskirts of Athens, was the ultimate ancestor of the modern university (hence the English term *academic*); an influential centre of research and learning, it attracted many men of outstanding ability. The great mathematicians Theaetetus (417–369 BCE) and Eudoxus of Cnidus (*c.* 395–*c.* 342 BCE) were associated with it. Although Plato was not a research mathematician, he was aware of the results of those who were, and he made use of them in his own work. For 20 years Aristotle was also a member of the Academy. He started his own school, the Lyceum, only after Plato's death, when he was passed over as Plato's successor at the Academy, probably because of his connections to the court of Macedonia, where he tutored Alexander the Great when the future emperor was a boy.

Because Aristotle often discusses issues by contrasting his views with those of his teacher, it is easy to be impressed by the ways in which they diverge. Thus, whereas for Plato the crown of ethics is the good in general, or Goodness itself (the Good), for Aristotle it is the good for human beings; and whereas for Plato the genus to which a thing belongs possesses a greater reality than the thing itself, for Aristotle the opposite is true. Plato's emphasis on the ideal, and Aristotle's on the worldly, informs Raphael's depiction of the two philosophers in the *School of Athens* (1508–11). But if one considers the two philosophers not just in relation to each other but in the context of the whole of Western philosophy, it is clear how much Aristotle's program is continuous with that of his teacher. (Indeed, the painting may be said to represent this continuity by showing the two men conversing amicably.) In any case, the Academy did not impose a dogmatic orthodoxy and in fact seems to have fostered a spirit of independent inquiry; at a later time it took on a skeptical orientation.

Raphael's School of Athens *shows Plato* (centre left) *and Aristotle* (centre right) *and symbolically explores the differences between them. Plato points to the heavens and the realm of forms, Aristotle to the earth and the realm of things.* Time & Life Pictures/Getty Images

DIALOGUE FORM

Glimpsed darkly even through translation's glass, Plato is a great literary artist. Yet he also made notoriously negative remarks about the value of writing. Similarly, although he believed that at least one of the purposes—if not the main purpose—of philosophy is to enable one to live a good life, by composing dialogues rather than treatises or hortatory letters he omitted to tell his readers directly any useful truths to live by.

One way of resolving these apparent tensions is to reflect on Plato's conception of philosophy. An important aspect of this conception, one that has been shared by many philosophers since Plato's time, is that philosophy aims not so much at discovering facts or establishing dogmas as at achieving wisdom or understanding. This wisdom or understanding is an extremely hard-won possession; it is no exaggeration to say that it is the result of a lifetime's effort, if it is achieved at all. Moreover, it is a possession that each person must win for himself. The writing or conversation of others may aid philosophical progress but cannot guarantee it. Contact with a living person, however, has certain advantages over an encounter with a piece of writing. As Plato pointed out, writing is limited by its fixity: it cannot modify itself to suit the individual reader or add anything new in response to queries. So it is only natural that Plato had limited expectations about what written works could achieve. On the other hand, he clearly did not believe that writing has no philosophical value. Written works still serve a purpose, as ways of interacting with inhabitants of times and places beyond the author's own and as a medium in which ideas can be explored and tested.

Dialogue form suits a philosopher of Plato's type. His use of dramatic elements, including humour, draws the reader in. Plato is unmatched in his ability to re-create the experience of conversation. The dialogues contain, in addition to Socrates and other authority figures, huge numbers of additional characters, some of whom act as representatives of certain classes of reader (as Glaucon may be a representative of talented and politically ambitious youth). These characters function not only to carry forward particular lines of thought but also to inspire readers to do the same—to join imaginatively in the discussion by constructing arguments and objections of their own. Spurring readers to philosophical activity is the primary purpose of the dialogues.

HAPPINESS AND VIRTUE

The characteristic question of ancient ethics is "How can I be happy?" and the most common answer to it is "by means of virtue." But in the relevant sense, happiness—the English translation of the ancient Greek *eudaimonia*—is not a mood or feeling but rather a condition of having things go well. Being happy amounts to living a life of human flourishing. Hence the question "How can I be happy?" is equivalent to "How can I live a good life?"

Whereas the notion of happiness in Greek philosophy applies at most to living things, that of *arete*—"virtue" or "excellence"—applies much more widely. Anything that has a characteristic use, function, or activity has a virtue or excellence, which is whatever disposition enables things of that kind to perform well. Human virtue, accordingly, is whatever enables human beings to live good lives. But it is far from obvious what a good life consists of, and so it is difficult to say what virtue might be.

Already by Plato's time a conventional set of virtues had come to be recognized by the larger culture; they included courage, justice, piety, modesty or temperance, and wisdom. Socrates and Plato undertook to discover what these virtues really amount to. A truly satisfactory account of any virtue would identify what it is, show how possessing it enables one to live well, and indicate how it is best acquired.

In Plato's representation of the activity of the historical Socrates, the interlocutors are examined in a search for definitions of the virtues. It is important to understand, however, that the definition sought for is not lexical, merely specifying what a speaker of the language would understand the term to mean as a matter of linguistic competence. Rather, the definition is one that gives an account of the real nature of the thing named by the term; accordingly, it is sometimes called a "real" definition. The real definition of *water*, for example, is H_2O, though speakers in most historical eras did not know this.

In the encounters Plato portrays, the interlocutors typically offer an example of the virtue they are asked to define (not the right kind of answer) or give a general account (the right kind of answer) that fails to accord with their intuitions on related matters. Socrates tends to suggest that virtue is not a matter of outward behaviour but is or involves a special kind of knowledge (knowledge of good and evil or knowledge of the use of other things).

The *Protagoras* addresses the question of whether the various commonly recognized virtues are different or really one. Proceeding from the interlocutor's assertion that the many have nothing to offer as their notion of the good besides pleasure, Socrates develops a picture of the agent according to which the great art necessary for a good human life is measuring and calculation; knowledge of the magnitudes of future pleasures and pains is all that is needed. If pleasure is the only object of desire, it seems unintelligible what, besides simple miscalculation, could cause anyone to behave badly. Thus the whole of virtue would consist of a certain kind of wisdom. The idea that knowledge is all that one needs for a good life, and that there is no aspect of character that is not reducible to cognition (and so no moral or emotional failure that is not a cognitive failure), is the characteristically Socratic position.

In the *Republic*, however, Plato develops a view of happiness and virtue that departs from that of Socrates. According to Plato, there are three parts of the soul, each with its own object of desire. Reason desires truth and the good of the whole individual, spirit is preoccupied with honour and competitive values, and appetite has the traditional low tastes for food, drink, and sex. Because the soul is complex, erroneous calculation is not the only way it can go wrong. The three parts can pull in different directions, and the low element, in a soul in which it is overdeveloped, can win out. Correspondingly, the good condition of the soul involves more than just cognitive excellence. In the terms of the *Republic*, the healthy or just soul has psychic harmony—the condition in which each of the three parts does its job properly. Thus, reason understands the Good in general and desires the actual good of the individual, and the other two parts of the soul desire what it is good for them to desire, so that spirit and appetite are activated by things that are healthy and proper.

Although the dialogue starts from the question "Why should I be just?," Socrates proposes that this inquiry can be advanced by examining justice "writ large" in an ideal city. Thus, the political discussion is undertaken to aid the ethical one. One early hint of the existence of the three parts of the soul in the individual is the existence of three classes in the well-functioning state: rulers, guardians, and producers. The wise state is the one in which the rulers understand the good; the courageous state is that in which the guardians can retain in the heat of battle the judgments handed down by the rulers about what is to be feared; the temperate state is that in which all citizens agree about who is to rule; and the just state is that in which each of the three classes does its own work properly. Thus, for the city to be fully virtuous, each citizen must contribute appropriately.

Justice as conceived in the *Republic* is so comprehensive that a person who possessed it would also possess all the other virtues, thereby achieving "the health of that whereby we live [the soul]." Yet, lest it be thought that habituation and correct instruction in human affairs alone can lead to this condition, one must keep in view that the *Republic* also develops the famous doctrine according to which reason cannot properly understand the human good or anything else without grasping the form of the Good itself. Thus the original inquiry, whose starting point was a motivation each individual is presumed to have (to learn how to live well), leads to a highly ambitious educational program. Starting with exposure only to salutary stories, poetry, and music from childhood and continuing with supervised habituation to good action and years of training in a series of mathematical disciplines, this program—and so virtue—would be complete only in the person who was able to grasp the first principle, the Good, and to proceed on that basis to secure accounts of the other realities. There are hints in the *Republic*, as well as in the tradition concerning Plato's lecture "On the Good" and in several of the more technical dialogues that this first principle is identical with Unity, or the One.

THE THEORY OF FORMS

Plato is both famous and infamous for his theory of forms. Just what the theory is, and whether it was ever viable, are matters of extreme controversy. To readers who approach Plato in English, the relationship between forms and sensible particulars, called in translation "participation," seems purposely mysterious. Moreover, the claim that the sensible realm is not fully real, and that it contrasts in this respect with the "pure being" of the forms, is perplexing. A satisfactory interpretation of the theory must rely on both historical knowledge and philosophical imagination.

LINGUISTIC AND PHILOSOPHICAL BACKGROUND

The terms that Plato uses to refer to forms, *idea* and *eidos*, ultimately derive from the verb *eidô*, "to look." Thus, an *idea* or *eidos* would be the look a thing presents, as when one speaks of a vase as having a lovely form. (Because the mentalistic connotation of *idea* in English is misleading—the *Parmenides* shows that forms cannot be ideas in a mind—this translation has fallen from favour.) Both terms can also be used in a more general sense to refer to any feature that two or more things have in common or to a kind of thing based on that feature. The English word *form* is similar. The sentence "The pottery comes in two forms" can be glossed as meaning either that the pottery is made in two shapes or that there are two kinds of pottery. When Plato wants to contrast genus with species, he tends to use the terms *genos* and *eidos*, translated as "genus" and "species," respectively. Although it is appropriate in the context to translate these as "genus" and "species," respectively, it is important not to lose sight of the continuity provided by the word *eidos*: even in these passages Plato is referring to the same kind of entities as always, the forms.

Another linguistic consideration that should be taken into account is the ambiguity of ancient Greek terms of the sort that would be rendered into unidiomatic English as "the dark" or "the beautiful." Such terms may refer to a particular individual that exhibits the feature in question, as when "the beautiful [one]" is used to refer to Achilles, but they may also refer to the features themselves, as when "the beautiful" is used to refer to something Achilles has. "The beautiful" in the latter usage may then be thought of as something general that all beautiful particulars have in common. In Plato's time, unambiguously abstract terms—corresponding to the English words "darkness" and "beauty"—came to be used as a way of avoiding the ambiguity inherent in the original terminology. Plato uses both kinds of terms.

By Plato's time there was also important philosophical precedent for using terms such as "the dark" and "the beautiful" to refer to metaphysically fundamental entities. Anaxagoras (c. 500–c. 428 BCE), the great pre-Socratic natural scientist, posited a long list of fundamental stuffs, holding that what are ordinarily understood as individuals are actually composites made up of shares or portions of these stuffs. The properties of sensible composites depend on which of their ingredients are predominant. Change, generation, and destruction in sensible particulars are conceived in terms of shifting combinations of portions of fundamental stuffs, which themselves are eternal and unchanging and accessible to the mind but not to the senses.

For Anaxagoras, having a share of something is straightforward: a particular composite possesses as a physical ingredient a material portion of the fundamental stuff in question. For example, a thing is observably hot because it possesses a sufficiently large portion of "the hot," which is thought of as the totality of heat in the world. The hot is itself hot, and this is why portions of it account for the warmth of composites. (In general, the fundamental stuffs posited by Anaxagoras themselves possessed the qualities they were supposed to account for in sensible particulars.) These portions are qualitatively identical to each other and to portions of the hot that are lost by whatever becomes less warm; they can move around the cosmos, being transferred from one composite to another, as heat may move from hot bathwater to Hector as it warms him up.

Plato's theory can be seen as a successor to that of Anaxagoras. Like Anaxagoras, Plato posits fundamental entities that are eternal and unchanging and accessible to the mind but not to the senses. And, as in Anaxagoras's theory, in Plato's theory sensible particulars display a given feature because they have a portion of the underlying thing itself. The Greek term used by both authors, *metechei*, is traditionally rendered as "participates in" in translations of Plato but as "has a portion of" in translations of Anaxagoras. This divergence has had the unfortunate effect of tending to hide from English-speaking readers that Plato is taking over a straightforward notion from his predecessor.

It is also possible to understand sympathetically the claim that forms have a greater reality than sensible particulars. The claim is certainly not that the sensible realm fails to exist or that it exists only partially or incompletely. Rather, sensibles are simply not ontologically or explanatorily basic: they are constituted of and explained by more fundamental entities, in Plato as in Anaxagoras (and indeed in most scientific theories). It is easy to multiply examples in the spirit of Plato to illustrate that adequate accounts of many of the fundamental entities he is interested in cannot be given in terms of sensible particulars or sensible properties. If someone who wishes to define beauty points at Helen of Troy, he points at a thing both beautiful (physically) and not beautiful (perhaps morally). Equally, if he specifies a sensible property like the gilded, he captures together things that are beautiful and things that are not. Sensible particulars and properties thus exhibit the phenomenon that Plato calls "rolling around between being and not-being": they are and are not x for values of x he is interested in (beautiful, just, equal, and so on). To understand beauty properly, one needs to capture something that is simply beautiful, however that is to be construed. The middle dialogues do not undertake to help the reader with this task.

Notice finally that because Plato was concerned with moral and aesthetic properties such as justice, beauty, and goodness, the Anaxagorean interpretation of participation—the idea that sensible composites are made up of physical portions of the fundamental entities—was not available to him. There is no qualitatively identical material constituent that a lyre gains as its sound becomes more beautiful and that Achilles loses as he ages. Plato's theory of forms would need a new interpretation of participation if it was to be carried out.

FORMS AS PERFECT EXEMPLARS

According to a view that some scholars have attributed to Plato's middle dialogues, participation is imitation or resemblance. Each form is approximated by the sensible particulars that display the property in question. Thus, Achilles and Helen are imperfect imitations of the Beautiful, which itself is maximally beautiful. On this interpretation, the "pure being" of the forms consists of their being perfect exemplars of themselves and not exemplars of anything else. Unlike Helen, the form of the Beautiful cannot be said to be both beautiful and not beautiful—similarly for Justice, Equality, and all the other forms.

This "super-exemplification" interpretation of participation provides a natural way of understanding the notion of the pure being of the forms and such self-predication sentences as "the Beautiful is beautiful." Yet it is absurd. In Plato's theory, forms play the functional role of universals, and most universals, such as greenness, generosity, and largeness, are not exemplars of themselves. (Greenness does not exhibit hue; generosity has no one to whom to give; largeness is not a gigantic object.) Moreover, it is problematic to require forms to exemplify only themselves, because there are properties, such as being and unity, that all things, including all forms, must exhibit. (So Largeness must have a share of Being to be anything at all, and it must have a share of Unity to be a single form.) Plato was not unaware of the severe difficulties inherent in the super-exemplification view; indeed, in the *Parmenides* and the *Sophist* he became the first philosopher to demonstrate these problems.

The first part of the *Parmenides* depicts the failure of the young Socrates to maintain the super-exemplification view of the forms against the critical examination of the older philosopher Parmenides. Since what Socrates there says about forms is reminiscent of the assertions of the character Socrates in the middle dialogues *Symposium*, *Phaedo*, and *Republic*, the exchange is usually interpreted as a negative assessment by Plato of the adequacy of his earlier presentation. Those who consider the first part of the *Parmenides* in isolation tend to suppose that Plato had heroically come to grips with the unviability of his theory, so that by his late period he was left with only dry and uninspiring exercises, divorced from the exciting program of the great masterpieces. Those who consider the dialogue as a whole, however, are encouraged by Parmenides' praise for the young Socrates and by his assertion that the exercise constituting the second part of the dialogue will help Socrates to get things right in the future. This suggests that Plato believed that the theory of forms could be developed in a way that would make it immune to the objections raised against the super-exemplification view.

FORMS AS GENERA AND SPECIES

Successful development of the theory of forms depended upon the development of a distinction between two kinds of predication. Plato held that a sentence making a predication about a sensible particular, "A is B," must be understood as stating that the particular in question, A, displays a certain property, B. There are ordinary predications about the forms, which also state that the forms in question display properties. Crucially, however, there is also a special kind of predication that can be used to express a form's nature. Since Plato envisaged that these natures could be given in terms of genus-species trees, a special predication about a form, "A is B," is true if B appears above A in its correct tree as a differentia or genus. Equivalently, "A is B" has the force that being a B is (part of) what it is to be an A. This special predication is closely approximated in modern classifications of animals and plants according to a biological taxonomy. "The wolf is a canis," for example, states that "wolf" appears below "canis" in a genus-species classification of the animals, or equivalently that being a canis is part of what it is to be a wolf (*Canis lupus*).

Plato's distinction can be illustrated by examples such as the following. The ordinary predication "Socrates is just" is true, because the individual in question displays the property of being just. Understood as a special predication, however, the assertion is false, because it is false that being just is part of what it is to be Socrates (there is no such thing as what it is to be Socrates). "Man is a vertebrate," understood as an ordinary predication, is false, since the form Man does not have a backbone. But when treated as a special predication it is true, since part of what it is to be a human is to be a vertebrate. Self-predication sentences are now revealed as trivial but true: "the Beautiful is beautiful" asserts only that being beautiful is (part of) what it is to be beautiful. In general one must be careful not to assume that Plato's self-predication sentences involve ordinary predication, which would in many cases involve problematic self-exemplification issues.

Plato was interested in special predication as a vehicle for providing the real definitions that he had been seeking in earlier dialogues. When one knows in this way what Justice itself really is, one can appreciate its relation to other entities of the same kind, including how it differs from the other virtues, such as Bravery, and whether it is really the whole of Virtue or only a part of it.

By means of special predication it is possible to provide an account of each fundamental nature. Such accounts, moreover, provide a way of understanding the "pure being" of the forms: it consists of the fact that there cannot be a true special predication of the form "A is both B and not-B." In other words, special predication sentences do not exhibit the phenomenon of rolling around between being and not being. This is because it must be the case that either B appears above A in a correct genus-species classification or it does not. Moreover, since forms do not function by being exemplars of themselves only, there is nothing to prevent their having other properties, such as being and unity, as appropriate. As Plato expresses it, all forms must participate in Being and Unity.

Because the special predications serve to give (in whole or in part) the real definitions that Socrates had been searching for, this interpretation of the forms connects Plato's most technical dialogues to the literary master-pieces and to the earlier Socratic dialogues. The technical works stress and develop the idea (which is hinted at in the early *Euthyphro*) that forms should be understood in terms of a genus-species classification. They develop a schema that, with modifications of course, went on to be productive in the work of Aristotle and many later researchers. In this way, Plato's late theory of the forms grows out of the program of his teacher and leads forward to the research of his students and well beyond.

THE DIALOGUES OF PLATO

Studies of both content and style have resulted in the division of Plato's works into three groups. Thus, (1) the early, or Socratic, dialogues represent conversations in which Socrates tests others on issues of human importance without discussing metaphysics; (2) the middle dialogues, or literary masterpieces, typically contain views originating with Plato on human issues, together with a sketch of a metaphysical position presented as foundational; and (3) the late dialogues, or technical studies, treat this metaphysical position in a fuller and more direct way. There are also some miscellaneous works, including letters, verses attributed to Plato, and dialogues of contested authenticity.

EARLY DIALOGUES

The works in this group (to be discussed in alphabetical order below) represent Plato's reception of the legacy of the historical Socrates; many feature his characteristic activity, *elenchos*, or testing of putative experts. The early dialogues serve well as an introduction to the corpus. They are short and entertaining and fairly accessible, even to readers with no background in philosophy. Indeed, they were probably intended by Plato to draw such readers into the subject. In them, Socrates typically engages a prominent contemporary about some facet of human excellence (virtue) that he is presumed to understand, but by the end of the conversation the participants are reduced to aporia. The discussion often includes as a core component a search for the real definition of a key term.

One way of reading the early dialogues is as having the primarily negative purpose of showing that authority figures in society do not have the understanding needed for a good human life (the reading of the skeptics in the Hellenistic Age). Yet there are other readings according to which the primary purpose is to recommend certain views. In Hellenistic times the Stoics regarded emphasis on the

A page from a 15th century Latin manuscript of Plato's dialogues. De Agostini Picture Library/Getty Images

paramount importance of virtue, understood as a certain kind of knowledge, as the true heritage of Socrates, and it became foundational for their school. Whether one prefers the skeptical or a more dogmatic interpretation of these dialogues, they function to introduce Plato's other works by clearing the ground; indeed, for this reason Plato's longer works sometimes include elenctic episodes as portions of themselves. Such episodes are intended to disabuse the naive, immature, or complacent reader of the comfortable conviction that he—or some authority figure in his community—already understands the deep issues in question and to convince him of the need for philosophical reflection on these matters.

The *Apology* represents the speech that Socrates gave in his defense at his trial, and it gives an interpretation of Socrates' career: he has been a "gadfly," trying to awaken the noble horse of Athens to an awareness of virtue, and he is wisest in the sense that he is aware that he knows nothing. Each of the other works in this group represents a particular Socratic encounter. In the *Charmides*, Socrates discusses temperance and self-knowledge with Critias and Charmides; at the fictional early date of the dialogue, Charmides is still a promising youth. The dialogue moves from an account in terms of behaviour ("temperance is a kind of quietness") to an attempt to specify the underlying state that accounts for it; the latter effort breaks down in puzzles over the reflexive application of knowledge.

The *Cratylus* (which some do not place in this group of works) discusses the question of whether names are correct by virtue of convention or nature. The *Crito* shows Socrates in prison, discussing why he chooses not to escape before the death sentence is carried out. The dialogue considers the source and nature of political obligation. The *Euthydemus* shows Socrates among the eristics (those who engage in showy logical disputation).

The *Euthyphro* asks, "What is piety?" Euthyphro fails to maintain the successive positions that piety is "what the gods love," "what the gods all love," or some sort of service to the gods. Socrates and Euthyphro agree that what they seek is a single form, present in all things that are pious, that makes them so. Socrates suggests that if Euthyphro could specify what part of justice piety is, he would have an account.

The more elaborate *Gorgias* considers, while its Sophist namesake is at Athens, whether orators command a genuine art or merely have a knack of flattery. Socrates holds that the arts of the legislator and the judge address the health of the soul, which orators counterfeit by taking the pleasant instead of the good as their standard. Discussion of whether one should envy the man who can bring about any result he likes leads to a Socratic paradox: it is better to suffer wrong than to do it. Callicles praises the man of natural ability who ignores conventional justice; true justice, according to Callicles, is this person's triumph. In the *Hippias Minor*, discussion of Homer by a visiting Sophist leads to an examination by Socrates, which the Sophist fails, on such questions as whether a just person who does wrong on purpose is better than other wrongdoers. The *Ion* considers professional reciters of poetry and develops the suggestion that neither such performers nor poets have any knowledge.

The interlocutors in the *Laches* are generals. One of them, the historical Laches, displayed less courage in the retreat from Delium (during the Peloponnesian War) than the humble foot soldier Socrates. Likewise, after the fictional date of the dialogue, another of the generals, Nicias, was responsible for the disastrous defeat of the Sicilian expedition because of his dependence on seers. Here the observation that the sons of great men often do not turn out well leads to an examination of what courage is. The trend again is from an account in terms of behaviour ("standing fast in battle") to an attempt to specify the inner state that underlies it ("knowledge of the grounds of hope and fear"), but none of the participants displays adequate understanding of these suggestions.

The *Lysis* is an examination of the nature of friendship; the work introduces the notion of a primary object of love, for whose sake one loves other things. The *Menexenus* purports to be a funeral oration that Socrates learned from Aspasia, the mistress of Pericles (himself celebrated for the funeral oration assigned to him by Thucydides, one of the most famous set pieces of Greek antiquity). This work may be a satire on the patriotic distortion of history.

The *Meno* takes up the familiar question of whether virtue can be taught, and, if so, why eminent men have not been able to bring up their sons to be virtuous. Concerned with method, the dialogue develops Meno's problem: how is it possible to search either for what one knows (for one already knows it) or for what one does not know (and so could not look for)? This is answered by the recollection theory of learning. What is called learning is really prompted recollection; one possesses all theoretical knowledge latently at birth, as demonstrated by the slave boy's ability to solve geometry problems when properly prompted. (This theory will reappear in the *Phaedo* and in the *Phaedrus*.) The dialogue is also famous as an early discussion of the distinction between knowledge and true belief.

The *Protagoras*, another discussion with a visiting Sophist, concerns whether virtue can be taught and whether the different virtues are really one. The dialogue contains yet another discussion of the phenomenon that the sons of the great are often undistinguished. This elaborate work showcases the competing approaches of the

Sophists (speechmaking, word analysis, discussion of great poetry) and Socrates. Under the guise of an interpretation of a poem of Simonides of Ceos (*c. 556–c. 468* BCE), a distinction (which will become thematic for Plato) is made between being and becoming. Most famously, this dialogue develops the characteristic Socratic suggestion that virtue is identical with wisdom and discusses the Socratic position that *akrasia* (moral weakness) is impossible. Socrates suggests that, in cases of apparent *akrasia*, what is really going on is an error of calculation: pursuing pleasure as the good, one incorrectly estimates the magnitude of the overall amount of pleasure that will result from one's action.

MIDDLE DIALOGUES

These longer, elaborate works are grouped together because of the similarity in their agendas: although they are primarily concerned with human issues, they also proclaim the importance of metaphysical inquiry and sketch Plato's proprietary views on the forms. This group represents the high point of Plato's literary artistry. Of course, each of Plato's finished works is an artistic success in the sense of being effectively composed in a way appropriate to its topic and its audience; yet this group possesses as well the more patent literary virtues. Typically much longer than the Socratic dialogues, these works contain sensitive portrayals of characters and their interactions, dazzling displays of rhetoric and attendant suggestions about its limitations, and striking and memorable tropes and myths, all designed to set off their leisurely explorations of philosophy.

In the middle dialogues, the character Socrates gives positive accounts, thought to originate with Plato himself, of the sorts of human issues that interlocutors in the earlier works had failed to grasp: the nature of Justice and the other virtues, Platonic love, and the soul (*psyche*). The works typically suggest that the desired understanding, to be properly grounded, requires more-fundamental inquiries, and so Socrates includes in his presentation a sketch of the forms. "Seeking the universal" by taking forms to be the proper objects of definition was already a hallmark of the early dialogues, though without attention to the status and character of these entities. Even the middle works, however, do not fully specify how the forms are to be understood.

At the party depicted in the *Symposium*, each of the guests (including the poets Aristophanes and Agathon) gives an encomium in praise of love. Socrates recalls the teaching of Diotima (a fictional prophetess), according to whom all mortal creatures have an impulse to achieve immortality. This leads to biological offspring with ordinary partners, but Diotima considers such offspring as poetry, scientific discoveries, and philosophy to be better. Ideally, one's eros (erotic love) should progress from ordinary love objects to Beauty itself. Alcibiades concludes the dialogue by bursting in and giving a drunken encomium of Socrates.

The *Phaedo* culminates in the affecting death of Socrates, before which he discusses a theme apposite to the occasion: the immortality of the soul (treated to some extent following Pythagorean and Orphic precedent). The dialogue features characteristically Platonic elements: the recollection theory of knowledge and the claim that understanding the forms is foundational to all else. The length of this work also accommodates a myth concerning the soul's career after death.

In the very long *Republic*, Socrates undertakes to show what Justice is and why it is in each person's best interest to be just. Initial concern for justice in the individual leads

Portions of a Classical manuscript of the Phaedo *by Plato, the oldest such manuscript of any considerable size.* British Library, London/HIP/Art Resource, NY

to a search for justice on a larger scale, as represented in an imaginary ideal city (hence the traditional title of the work). In the Republic the rulers and guardians are forbidden to have private families or property, women perform the same tasks as men, and the rulers are philosophers—those who have knowledge of the Good and the Just. The dialogue contains two discussions—one with each of Plato's brothers—of the impact of art on moral development. Socrates develops the proposal that Justice in a city or an individual is the condition in which each part performs the task that is proper to it; such an entity will have no motivation to do unjust acts and will be free of internal conflict. The soul consists of reason, spirit, and appetite, just as the city consists of rulers, guardians, and craftsmen or producers.

The middle books of the *Republic* contain a sketch of Plato's views on knowledge and reality and feature the famous figures of the Sun and the Cave, among others. The position occupied by the form of the Good in the intelligible world is the same as that occupied by the Sun in the visible world: thus the Good is responsible for the being and intelligibility of the objects of thought. The usual cognitive condition of human beings is likened to that of prisoners chained in an underground cave, with a great fire behind them and a raised wall in between. The prisoners are chained in position and so are able to see only shadows cast on the facing wall by statues moved along the wall behind them. They take these shadows to be reality. The account of the progress that they would achieve if they were to go above ground and see the real world in the light of the Sun features the notion of knowledge as enlightenment. Plato proposes a concrete sequence of mathematical studies, ending with harmonics, that would prepare future rulers to engage in dialectic, whose task is to say of each thing what it is—i.e., to specify its nature by giving a real definition. Contrasting with the portrait of the just man and the city are those of decadent types of personality and regime. The dialogue concludes with a myth concerning the fate of souls after death.

The first half of the *Phaedrus* consists of competitive speeches of seduction. Socrates repents of his first attempt and gives a treatment of love as the impulse to philosophy: Platonic love, as in the *Symposium*, is eros, here graphically described. The soul is portrayed as made of a white horse (noble), a black horse (base), and a charioteer; Socrates provides an elaborate description of the soul's discarnate career as a spectator of the vision of the forms, which it may recall in this life. Later in the dialogue, Socrates maintains that philosophical knowledge is necessary to an effective rhetorician, who produces likenesses of truth adapted to his audience (and so must know both the truth concerning the subject matter and the receptivities of different characters to different kinds of presentation). This part of the dialogue, with its developed interest in genera and species, looks forward to the group of technical studies. It is also notable for its discussion of the limited value of writing.

LATE DIALOGUES

The *Parmenides* demonstrates that the sketches of forms presented in the middle dialogues were not adequate; this dialogue and the ones that follow spur readers to develop a more viable understanding of these entities. Thus, the approach to genera and species recommended in the *Sophist*, the *Statesman*, and the *Philebus* (and already discussed in the *Phaedrus*) represents the late version of Plato's theory of forms. The *Philebus* proposes a mathematized version, inspired by Pythagoreanism and corresponding to the cosmology of the *Timaeus*.

But Plato did not neglect human issues in these dialogues. The *Phaedrus* already combined the new apparatus with a compelling treatment of love; the title topics of the *Sophist* and the *Statesman*, to be treated by genus-species division, are important roles in the Greek city; and the *Philebus* is a consideration of the competing claims of pleasure and knowledge to be the basis of the good life. (The *Laws*, left unfinished at Plato's death, seems to represent a practical approach to the planning of a city.) If one combines the hints (in the *Republic*) associating the Good with the One, or Unity; the treatment (in the *Parmenides*) of the One as the first principle of everything; and the possibility that the good proportion and harmony featured in the *Timaeus* and the *Philebus* are aspects of the One, it is possible to trace the aesthetic and ethical interests of the middle dialogues through even the most difficult technical studies.

The *Theaetetus* considers the question "What is knowledge?" Is it perception, true belief, or true belief with an "account"? The dialogue contains a famous "digression" on the difference between the philosophical and worldly mentalities. The work ends inconclusively and may indeed be intended to show the limits of the methods of the historical Socrates with this subject matter, further progress requiring Plato's distinctive additions.

The *Parmenides* is the key episode in Plato's treatment of forms. It presents a critique of the super-exemplification view of forms that results from a natural reading of the *Symposium*, the *Phaedo*, and the *Republic* and moves on to a suggestive logical exercise based on a distinction between two kinds of predication and a model of the forms in terms of genera and species. Designed to lead the reader to a more sophisticated and viable theory, the exercise also depicts the One as a principle of everything.

The leader of the discussion in the *Sophist* is an "Eleatic stranger." Sophistry seems to involve trafficking in falsity, illusion, and not-being. Yet these are puzzling in light of the brilliant use by the historical Parmenides (also an Eleatic) of the slogan that one cannot think or speak of what is not. Plato introduces the idea that a negative assertion of the form "A is not B" should be understood not as invoking any absolute not-being but as having the force that A is other than B. The other crucial content of the dialogue is its distinction between two uses of "is," which correspond to the two kinds of predication introduced in the *Parmenides*. Both are connected with the genus-species model of definition that is pervasive in the late dialogues, since the theoretically central use of "is" appears in statements that are true in virtue of the relations represented in genus-species classifications. The dialogue treats the intermingling of the five "greatest kinds": Being, Sameness, Difference, Motion, and Rest. Although these kinds are of course not species of each other, they do partake of each other in the ordinary way. The *Statesman* discusses genus-species definition in connection with understanding its title notion.

The *Timaeus* concerns the creation of the world by a Demiurge, initially operating on forms and space and assisted after he has created them by lesser gods. Earth, air, fire, and water are analyzed as ultimately consisting of two kinds of triangles, which combine into different characteristic solids. Plato in this work applies mathematical harmonics to produce a cosmology. The *Critias* is a barely started sequel to the *Timaeus*; its projected content is the story of the war of ancient Athens and Atlantis.

The *Philebus* develops major apparatuses in methodology and metaphysics. The genus-species treatment of forms is recommended, but now foundational to it is a new fourfold division: limit, the unlimited, the mixed class, and the cause. Forms (members of the mixed class) are analyzed in Pythagorean style as made up of limit and the unlimited. This occurs when desirable ratios govern the balance between members of underlying pairs of opposites—as, for example, Health results when there is a proper balance between the Wet and the Dry.

The very lengthy *Laws* is thought to be Plato's last composition, since there is generally accepted evidence that it was unrevised at his death. It develops laws to govern a projected state and is apparently meant to be practical in a way that the *Republic* was not; thus the demands made on human nature are less exacting. This work appears, indirectly, to have left its mark on the great system of Roman jurisprudence.

CHAPTER 4

THE PHILOSOPHY OF ARISTOTLE

The thought of Aristotle determined the course of Western intellectual history for more than two millenia. He is generally regarded as one of the two greatest philosophers who ever lived, the other being his teacher, Plato.

HIS LIFE

THE ACADEMY

Aristotle was born on the Chalcidic peninsula of Macedonia, in northern Greece, in 384 BCE; he died in 322 in Chalcis, on the island of Euboea. His father, Nicomachus, was the physician of Amyntas III (reigned *c.* 393–*c.* 370 BCE), king of Macedonia and grandfather of Alexander the Great (reigned 336–323 BCE). After his father's death in 367, Aristotle migrated to Athens, where he joined the Academy of Plato. He remained there for 20 years as Plato's pupil and colleague.

Many of Plato's later dialogues date from these decades, and they may reflect Aristotle's contributions to philosophical debate at the Academy. Some of Aristotle's writings also belong to this period, though mostly they survive only in fragments. Like his master,

Aristotle wrote initially in dialogue form, and his early ideas show a strong Platonic influence. His dialogue *Eudemus*, for example, reflects the Platonic view of the soul as imprisoned in the body and as capable of a happier life only when the body has been left behind. According to Aristotle, the dead are more blessed and happier than the living, and to die is to return to one's real home.

Another youthful work, the *Protrepticus* ("Exhortation"), has been reconstructed by modern

Aristotle, marble bust with a restored nose, Roman copy of a Greek original, last quarter of the 4th century BCE. In the Kunsthistorisches Museum, Vienna. Courtesy of the Kunsthistorisches Museum, Vienna

scholars from quotations in various works from late antiquity. Everyone must do philosophy, Aristotle claims, because even arguing against the practice of philosophy is itself a form of philosophizing. The best form of philosophy is the contemplation of the universe of nature; it is for this purpose that God made human beings and gave them a godlike intellect. All else—strength, beauty, power, and honour—is worthless.

It is possible that two of Aristotle's surviving works on logic and disputation, the *Topics* and the *Sophistical Refutations*, belong to this early period. The former demonstrates how to construct arguments for a position one has already decided to adopt; the latter shows how to detect weaknesses in the arguments of others. Although neither work amounts to a systematic treatise on formal logic, Aristotle can justly say, at the end of the *Sophistical Refutations*, that he has invented the discipline of logic— nothing at all existed when he started.

During Aristotle's residence at the Academy, King Philip II of Macedonia (reigned 359–336 BCE) waged war on a number of Greek city-states. The Athenians defended their independence only half-heartedly, and, after a series of humiliating concessions, they allowed Philip to become, by 338, master of the Greek world. It cannot have been an easy time to be a Macedonian resident in Athens.

Within the Academy, however, relations seem to have remained cordial. Aristotle always acknowledged a great debt to Plato; he took a large part of his philosophical agenda from Plato, and his teaching is more often a modification than a repudiation of Plato's doctrines. Already, however, Aristotle was beginning to distance himself from Plato's theory of Forms, or Ideas (*eidos*). Plato had held that, in addition to particular things, there exists a suprasensible realm of Forms, which are immutable and everlasting. This realm, he maintained, makes particular things intelligible by accounting for their common natures: a thing is a horse, for example, by virtue of the fact that it shares in, or imitates, the Form of "Horse." In a lost work, *On Ideas*, Aristotle maintains that the arguments of Plato's central dialogues establish only that there are, in addition to particulars, certain common objects of the sciences. In his surviving works as well, Aristotle often takes issue with the theory of Forms, sometimes politely and sometimes contemptuously. In his *Metaphysics* he argues that the theory fails to solve the problems it was meant to address. It does not confer intelligibility on particulars, because immutable and everlasting Forms cannot explain how particulars come into existence and undergo change. All the theory does, according to Aristotle, is introduce new entities equal in number to the entities to be explained—as if one could solve a problem by doubling it.

TRAVELS

When Plato died about 348, his nephew Speusippus became head of the Academy, and Aristotle left Athens. He migrated to Assus, a city on the northwestern coast of Anatolia (in present-day Turkey), where Hermias, a graduate of the Academy, was ruler. Aristotle became a close friend of Hermias and eventually married his ward Pythias. Aristotle helped Hermias to negotiate an alliance with Macedonia, which angered the Persian king, who had Hermias treacherously arrested and put to death. Aristotle saluted Hermias's memory in *Ode to Virtue,* his only surviving poem.

While in Assus and during the subsequent few years when he lived in the city of Mytilene on the island of Lesbos, Aristotle carried out extensive scientific research, particularly in zoology and marine biology. This work was summarized in a book later known, misleadingly, as *The History of Animals,* to which Aristotle added two short treatises, *On the Parts of Animals* and *On the Generation of Animals.* Although Aristotle did not claim to have founded the science of zoology, his detailed observations of a wide variety of organisms were quite without precedent. He— or one of his research assistants—must have been gifted with remarkably acute eyesight, since some of the features of insects that he accurately reports were not again observed until the invention of the microscope in the 17th century.

The scope of Aristotle's scientific research is astonishing. Much of it is concerned with the classification of animals into genus and species; more than 500 species figure in his treatises, many of them described in detail. The myriad items of information about the anatomy, diet, habitat, modes of copulation, and reproductive systems of mammals, reptiles, fish, and insects are a melange of minute investigation and vestiges of superstition. In some cases his unlikely stories about rare species of fish were proved accurate many centuries later. In other places he states clearly and fairly a biological problem that took millennia to solve, such as the nature of embryonic development.

Despite an admixture of the fabulous, Aristotle's biological works must be regarded as a stupendous achievement. His inquiries were conducted in a genuinely scientific spirit, and he was always ready to confess ignorance where evidence was insufficient. Whenever there is a conflict between theory and observation, one must trust observation, he insisted, and theories are to be trusted only if their results conform with the observed phenomena.

About eight years after the death of Hermias, in 343 or 342, Aristotle was summoned by Philip II to the Macedonian capital at Pella to act as tutor to Philip's 13-year-old son, the future Alexander the Great. Little is known of the content of Aristotle's instruction; although the *Rhetoric to Alexander* was included in the Aristotelian corpus for centuries, it is now commonly regarded as a forgery. By 326 Alexander had made himself master of an empire that stretched from the Danube to the Indus and included Libya and Egypt. Ancient sources report that during his campaigns Alexander arranged for biological specimens to be sent to his tutor from all parts of Greece and Asia Minor.

Aristotle (right) *teaches Philip II of Macedonia's son, who would go on to become Alexander the Great.* Bibliothéque Nationale, Paris, France/The Bridgeman Art Library/Getty Images

THE LYCEUM

While Alexander was conquering Asia, Aristotle, now 50 years old, was in Athens. Just outside the city boundary, in a grove sacred to Apollo Lyceius (so called because he protected the flocks from wolves [*lykoi*]), he established his own school, known as the Lyceum. He built a very substantial library and gathered around him a group of brilliant research students, called "peripatetics" from the name of the cloister (*peripatos*) in which they walked and held their discussions. The Lyceum was not a private club

Archaeologists believe the ruins above to have once been part of Aristotle's Lyceum. © AP Images

like the Academy; many of the lectures there were open to the general public and given free of charge.

Most of Aristotle's surviving works, with the exception of the zoological treatises, probably belong to this second Athenian sojourn. There is no certainty about their chronological order, and indeed it is probable that the main treatises—on physics, metaphysics, psychology, ethics, and politics—were constantly rewritten and updated. Every proposition of Aristotle is fertile of ideas and full of energy, though his prose is commonly neither lucid nor elegant.

Aristotle's works, though not as polished as Plato's, are systematic in a way that Plato's never were. Plato's dialogues shift constantly from one topic to another, always (from a modern perspective) crossing the boundaries between different philosophical or scientific disciplines. Indeed, there was no such thing as an intellectual discipline until Aristotle invented the notion during his Lyceum period.

Aristotle divided the sciences into three kinds: productive, practical, and theoretical. The productive sciences, naturally enough, are those that have a product. They include not only engineering and architecture, which have products like bridges and houses, but also disciplines such as strategy and rhetoric, where the product is something less concrete, such as victory on the battlefield or in the courts. The practical sciences, most notably ethics and politics, are those that guide behaviour. The theoretical sciences are those that have no product and no practical goal but in which information and understanding are sought for their own sake.

During Aristotle's years at the Lyceum, his relationship with his former pupil Alexander apparently cooled. Alexander became more and more megalomaniac, finally proclaiming himself divine and demanding that Greeks prostrate themselves before him in adoration. Opposition to this demand was led by Aristotle's nephew Callisthenes (*c.* 360–327 BCE), who had been appointed historian of Alexander's Asiatic expedition on Aristotle's recommendation. For his heroism Callisthenes was falsely implicated in a plot and executed.

When Alexander died in 323, democratic Athens became uncomfortable for Macedonians, even those who were anti-imperialist. Saying that he did not wish the city that had executed Socrates "to sin twice against philosophy," Aristotle fled to Chalcis, where he died the following year. His will, which survives, makes thoughtful provision for a large number of friends and dependents. To Theophrastus (*c.* 372–*c.* 287 BCE), his successor as head of the Lyceum, he left his library, including his own writings, which were vast. Aristotle's surviving works amount to about one million words, though they probably represent only about one-fifth of his total output.

HIS PHILOSOPHY

LOGIC

Aristotle's claim to be the founder of logic rests primarily on the *Categories*, the *De interpretatione*, and the *Prior Analytics*, which deal respectively with words, propositions, and syllogisms. These works, along with the *Topics*, the *Sophistical Refutations*, and a treatise on scientific method, the *Posterior Analytics*, were grouped together in a collection known as the *Organon*, or "tool" of thought.

SYLLOGISTIC

The *Prior Analytics* is devoted to the theory of the syllogism, a central method of inference that can be illustrated by familiar examples such as the following:

Every Greek is human. Every human is mortal. Therefore, every Greek is mortal.

Aristotle discusses the various forms that syllogisms can take and identifies which forms constitute reliable inferences. The example above contains three propositions in the indicative mood, which Aristotle calls "propositions." (Roughly speaking, a proposition is a proposition considered solely with respect to its logical features.) The third proposition, the one beginning with "therefore," Aristotle calls the conclusion of the syllogism. The other two propositions may be called premises, though Aristotle does not consistently use any particular technical term to distinguish them.

The propositions in the example above begin with the word *every*; Aristotle calls such propositions "universal." (In English, universal propositions can be expressed by using *all* rather than *every*; thus, *Every Greek is human* is equivalent to *All Greeks are human*.) Universal propositions may be affirmative, as in this example, or negative, as in *No Greek is a horse*. Universal propositions differ from "particular" propositions, such as *Some Greek is bearded* (a particular affirmative) and *Some Greek is not bearded* (a particular negative). In the Middle Ages it became customary to call the difference between universal and particular propositions a difference of "quantity" and the difference between affirmative and negative propositions a difference of "quality."

In propositions of all these kinds, Aristotle says, something is predicated of something else. The items that enter into predications Aristotle calls "terms." It is a feature of terms, as conceived by Aristotle, that they can figure either as predicates or as subjects of predication. This means that they can play three distinct roles in a syllogism. The term that is the predicate of the conclusion is the "major" term; the term of which the major term is predicated in the conclusion is the "minor" term; and the term that appears in each of the premises is the "middle" term.

In addition to inventing this technical vocabulary, Aristotle introduced the practice of using schematic letters to identify particular patterns of argument, a device that is essential for the systematic study of inference and that is ubiquitous in modern mathematical logic. Thus, the pattern of argument exhibited in the example above can be represented in the schematic proposition:

> *If A belongs to every B, and B belongs to every C, A belongs to every C.*

Because propositions may differ in quantity and quality, and because the middle term may occupy several different places in the premises, many different patterns of syllogistic inference are possible. Additional examples are the following:

> *Every Greek is human. No human is immortal. Therefore, no Greek is immortal.*
> *Some animal is a dog. Some dog is white. Therefore, every animal is white.*

From late antiquity, triads of these different kinds were called "moods" of the syllogism. The two moods illustrated above exhibit an important difference: the first is a valid argument, and the second is an invalid argument, having true premises and a false conclusion. An argument is valid only if its form is such that it will never lead from true premises to a false conclusion. Aristotle sought to determine which forms result in valid inferences. He set out a number of rules giving necessary conditions for the validity of a syllogism, such as the following:

At least one premise must be universal.
At least one premise must be affirmative.
If either premise is negative, the conclusion must be negative.

Aristotle's syllogistic is a remarkable achievement: it is a systematic formulation of an important part of logic. From roughly the Renaissance until the early 19th century, it was widely believed that syllogistic was the whole of logic. But in fact it is only a fragment. It does not deal, for example, with inferences that depend on words such as *and*, *or*, and *if . . . then*, which, instead of attaching to nouns, link whole propositions together.

PROPOSITIONS AND CATEGORIES

Aristotle's writings show that even he realized that there is more to logic than syllogistic. The *De interpretatione*, like the *Prior Analytics*, deals mainly with general propositions beginning with *Every*, *No*, or *Some*. But its main concern is not to link these propositions to each other in syllogisms but to explore the relations of compatibility and incompatibility between them. *Every swan is white* and *No swan is white* clearly cannot both be true; Aristotle calls such pairs of propositions "contraries." They can, however, both be false, if—as is the case—some swans are white and some are not. *Every swan is white* and *Some swan is not white*, like the former pair, cannot both be true, but—on the assumption that there are such things as swans—they cannot both be false either. If one of them is true, the other is false; and if one of them is false, the other is true. Aristotle calls such pairs of propositions "contradictories."

The propositions that enter into syllogisms are all general propositions, whether universal or particular; that is to say, none of them is a proposition about an individual, containing a proper name, such as the proposition *Socrates is wise*. To find a systematic treatment of singular propositions, one must turn to the *Categories*. This treatise begins by dividing the "things that are said" (the expressions of speech) into those that are simple and those that are complex. Examples of complex sayings are *A man runs, A woman speaks*, and *An ox drinks*; simple sayings are the particular words that enter into such complexes: *man, runs, woman, speaks*, and so on. Only complex sayings can be statements, true or false; simple sayings are neither true nor false. The *Categories* identifies 10 different ways in which simple expressions may signify; these are the categories that give the treatise its name. To introduce the categories, Aristotle employs a heterogeneous set of expressions, including nouns (e.g., *substance*), verbs (e.g., *wearing*), and interrogatives (e.g., *where?* or *how big?*). By the Middle Ages it had become customary to refer to each category by a more or less abstract noun: substance, quantity, quality, relation, place, time, posture, vesture, activity, and passivity.

The categories are intended as a classification of both the kinds of expression that may function as a predicate in a proposition and of the kinds of extralinguistic entity such expressions may signify. One might say of Socrates, for example, that he was human (substance), that he was five feet tall (quantity), that he was wise (quality), that he was older than Plato (relation), and that he lived in Athens (place) in the 5th century BCE (time). On a particular occasion, his friends might have said of him that he was sitting (posture), wearing a cloak (vesture), cutting a piece of cloth (activity), or being warmed by the sun (passivity).

If one follows Aristotle's lead, one will easily be able to classify the predicates in propositions such as *Socrates is potbellied* and *Socrates is wiser than Meletus*. But what about the term *Socrates* in propositions such as *Socrates is human?* What category does it belong to? Aristotle answers the question by making a distinction between "first substance" and "second substance." In *Socrates is human, Socrates* refers to a first substance—an individual—and *human* to a second substance—a species or kind. Thus, the proposition predicates the species human of an individual, Socrates.

Aristotle's logical writings contain two different conceptions of the structure of a proposition and the nature of its parts. One conception can trace its ancestry to Plato's dialogue the *Sophist*. In that work Plato introduces a distinction between nouns and verbs, a verb being the sign of an action and a noun being the sign of an agent of an action. A proposition, he claims, must consist of at least one noun and at least one verb; two nouns in succession or two verbs in succession—as in *lion stag* and *walks runs*—will never make a proposition. The simplest kind of proposition is something like *A man learns* or *Theaetetus flies*, and only something with this kind of structure can be true or false. It is this conception of a proposition as constructed from two quite heterogeneous elements that is to the fore in the *Categories* and the *De interpretatione*, and it is also paramount in modern logic.

In the syllogistic of the *Prior Analytics*, in contrast, the proposition is conceived in quite a different way. The basic elements out of which it is constructed are terms, which are not heterogeneous like nouns and verbs but can occur indifferently, without change of meaning, as either subjects or predicates. One flaw in the doctrine of terms is that it fosters confusion between signs and what they signify. In the proposition *Every human is mortal*, for example, is *mortal* predicated of humans or of *human?* It is important to distinguish between use and mention—between the use of a word to talk about what it signifies and the mention of a word to talk about the word itself. This distinction was not always easy to make in ancient Greek, because the language lacked quotation marks. There is no doubt that Aristotle sometimes fell into confusion between use and mention; the wonder is that, given his dysfunctional doctrine of terms, he did not do so more often.

PHYSICS AND METAPHYSICS

Aristotle divided the theoretical sciences into three groups: physics, mathematics, and theology. Physics as he understood it was equivalent to what would now be called "natural philosophy," or the study of nature (*physis*); in this sense it encompasses not only the modern field of physics but also biology, chemistry, geology, psychology, and even meteorology. Metaphysics, or the philosophical study whose object is to determine the ultimate nature of reality, however, is notably absent from Aristotle's classification; indeed, he never uses the word, which first appears in the posthumous catalog of his writings as a name for the works listed after the *Physics*. He does, however, recognize the branch of philosophy now called metaphysics: he calls it "first philosophy" and defines it as the discipline that studies "being as being."

Aristotle's contributions to the physical sciences are less impressive than his researches in the life sciences. In works such as *On Generation and Corruption* and *On the Heavens*, he presented a world-picture that included many features inherited from his pre-Socratic predecessors. From Empedocles (*c.* 490–430 BCE) he adopted the view that the universe is ultimately composed of different combinations of the four fundamental elements of earth, water, air, and fire. Each element is characterized by the possession of a unique pair of the four elementary qualities of heat, cold, wetness, and dryness: earth is cold and dry, water is cold and wet, air is hot and wet, and fire is hot and dry. Each element has a natural place in an ordered cosmos, and each has an innate tendency to move toward this natural place. Thus, earthy solids naturally fall, while fire, unless prevented, rises ever higher. Other motions of the elements are possible but are "violent." (A relic of Aristotle's distinction is preserved in the modern-day contrast between natural and violent death.)

Aristotle's vision of the cosmos also owes much to Plato's dialogue *Timaeus*. As in that work, the Earth is at the centre of the universe, and around it the Moon, the Sun, and the other planets revolve in a succession of concentric crystalline spheres. The heavenly bodies are not compounds of the four terrestrial elements but are made up of a superior fifth element, or "quintessence." In addition, the heavenly bodies have souls, or supernatural intellects, which guide them in their travels through the cosmos.

Even the best of Aristotle's scientific work has now only a historical interest. The abiding value of treatises such as the *Physics* lies not in their particular scientific assertions but in their philosophical analyses of some of the concepts that pervade the physics of different eras — concepts such as place, time, causation, and determinism.

PLACE

Every body appears to be in some place, and every body (at least in principle) can move from one place to another. The same place can be occupied at different times by different bodies, as a flask can contain first wine and then air. So a place cannot be identical to the body that occupies it. What, then, is place? According to Aristotle, the place of a thing is the first motionless boundary of whatever body is containing it. Thus, the place of a pint of wine is the inner surface of the flask containing it—provided the flask is stationary. But suppose the flask is in motion, perhaps on a punt floating down a river. Then the wine will be moving too, from place to place, and its place must be given by specifying its position relative to the motionless river banks.

As is clear from this example, for Aristotle a thing is not only in the place defined by its immediate container but also in whatever contains that container. Thus, all human beings are not only on the Earth but also in the universe; the universe is the place that is common to everything. But the universe itself is not in a place at all, since it has no container outside it. Thus, it is clear that place as described by Aristotle is quite different from space as conceived by Isaac Newton (1643–1727)—as an infinite extension or cosmic grid. Newtonian space would exist whether or not the material universe had been created. For Aristotle, if there were no bodies, there would be no place. Aristotle does, however, allow for the existence of a vacuum, or "void," but only if it is contained by actually existing bodies.

THE CONTINUUM

Spacial extension, motion, and time are often thought of as continua—as wholes made up of a series of smaller parts. Aristotle develops a subtle analysis of the nature of such continuous quantities. Two entities are continuous, he says, when there is only a single common boundary between them. On the basis of this definition, he seeks to show that a continuum cannot be composed of indivisible atoms. A line, for example, cannot be composed of points that lack magnitude. Since a point has no parts, it cannot have a boundary distinct from itself; two points, therefore, cannot be either adjacent or continuous. Between any two points on a continuous line there will always be other points on the same line.

Similar reasoning, Aristotle says, applies to time and to motion. Time cannot be composed of indivisible moments, because between any two moments there is always a period of time. Likewise, an atom of motion would in fact have to be an atom of rest. Moments or points that were indivisible would lack magnitude, and zero magnitude, however often repeated, can never add up to any magnitude.

Any magnitude, then, is infinitely divisible. But this means "unendingly divisible," not "divisible into infinitely many parts." However often a magnitude has been divided, it can always be divided further. It is infinitely divisible in the sense that there is no end to its divisibility. The continuum does not have an infinite number of parts; indeed, Aristotle regarded the idea of an actually infinite number as incoherent. The infinite, he says, has only a "potential" existence.

MOTION

Motion (*kinesis*) was for Aristotle a broad term, encompassing changes in several different categories. A paradigm of his theory of motion, which appeals to the key notions of actuality and potentiality, is local motion, or movement from place to place. If a body X is to move from point A to point B, it must be able to do so: when it is at A it is only potentially at B. When this potentiality has been realized, then X is at B. But it is then at rest and not in motion. So motion from A to B is not simply the actualization of a potential at A for being at B. Is it then a partial actualization of that potentiality? That will not do either, because a body stationary at the midpoint between A and B might be said to have partially actualized that potentiality. One must say that motion is an actualization of a potentiality that is still being actualized. In the *Physics*

Aristotle accordingly defines motion as "the actuality of what is in potentiality, insofar as it is in potentiality."

Motion is a continuum: a mere series of positions between A and B is not a motion from A to B. If X is to move from A to B, however, it must pass through any intermediate point between A and B. But passing through a point is not the same as being located at that point. Aristotle argues that whatever is in motion has already been in motion. If X, traveling from A to B, passes through the intermediate point K, it must have already passed through an earlier point J, intermediate between A and K. But however short the distance between A and J, that too is divisible, and so on ad infinitum. At any point at which X is moving, therefore, there will be an earlier point at which it was already moving. It follows that there is no such thing as a first instant of motion.

TIME

For Aristotle, extension, motion, and time are three fundamental continua in an intimate and ordered relation to each other. Local motion derives its continuity from the continuity of extension, and time derives its continuity from the continuity of motion. Time, Aristotle says, is the number of motion with respect to before and after. Where there is no motion, there is no time. This does not imply that time is identical with motion: motions are motions of particular things, and different kinds of changes are motions of different kinds, but time is universal and uniform. Motions, again, may be faster or slower; not so time. Indeed, it is by the time they take that the speed of motions is determined. Nonetheless, Aristotle says, "we perceive motion and time together." One observes how much time has passed by observing the process of some change. In particular, for Aristotle, the days, months, and years are measured by observing the Sun, the Moon, and the stars upon their celestial travels.

The part of a journey that is nearer its starting point comes before the part that is nearer its end. The spatial relation of nearer and farther underpins the relation of before and after in motion, and the relation of before and after in motion underpins the relation of earlier and later in time. Thus, on Aristotle's view, temporal order is ultimately derived from the spatial ordering of stretches of motion.

MATTER

Change, for Aristotle, can take place in many different categories. Local motion, as noted above, is change in the category of place. Change in the category of quantity is growth (or shrinkage), and change in the category of quality (e.g., of colour) is what Aristotle calls "alteration." Change in the category of substance, however—a change of one kind of thing into another—is very special. When a substance undergoes a change of quantity or quality, the same substance remains throughout. But does anything persist when one kind of thing turns into another? Aristotle's answer is yes: matter. He says,

> By matter, I mean what in itself is neither of any kind nor of any size nor describable by any of the categories of being. For it is something of which all these things are predicated, and therefore its essence is different from that of all the predicates.

An entity that is not of any kind, size, or shape and of which nothing at all can be said may seem highly mysterious, but this is not what Aristotle has in mind. His ultimate matter (he sometimes calls it "prime matter") is not in itself of any kind. It is not in itself of any particular size, because it can grow or shrink; it is not in itself water or steam, because it is both of these in turn. But this does not mean that there is any time at which it is not of any size or any time at which it is neither water nor steam nor anything else.

Ordinary life provides many examples of pieces of matter changing from one kind to another. A bottle containing a pint of cream may be found, after shaking, to contain not cream but butter. The stuff that comes out of the bottle is the same as the stuff that went into it; nothing has been added and nothing taken away. But what comes out is different in kind from what went in. It is from cases such as this that the Aristotelian notion of matter is derived.

FORM

Although Aristotle's system makes room for forms, they differ significantly from Forms as Plato conceived them. For Aristotle, the form of a particular thing is not separate (*chorista*) from the thing itself—any form is the form of some thing. In Aristotle's physics, form is always paired with matter, and the paradigm examples of forms are those of material substances.

Aristotle distinguishes between "substantial" and "accidental" forms. A substantial form is a second substance (species or kind) considered as a universal; the predicate *human*, for example, is universal as well as substantial. Thus, *Socrates is human* may be described as predicating a second substance of a first substance (Socrates) or as predicating a substantial form of a first substance. Whereas substantial forms correspond to the category of substance, accidental forms correspond to categories other than substance; they are nonsubstantial categories considered as universals. *Socrates is wise*, for example, may be described as predicating a quality (*wise*) of a first substance or as predicating an accidental form of a first substance. Aristotle calls such forms "accidental" because they may undergo change, or be gained or lost, without thereby changing the first substance into something else or causing it to cease to exist. Substantial forms, in contrast, cannot be gained or lost without changing the nature of the substance of which they are predicated. In the propositions above, *wise* is an accidental form and *human* a substantial form; Socrates could survive the loss of the former but not the loss of the latter.

When a thing comes into being, neither its matter nor its form is created. When one manufactures a bronze sphere, for example, what comes into existence is not the bronze or the spherical shape but the shaped bronze. Similarly in the case of the human Socrates. But the fact that the forms of things are not created does not mean that they must exist independently of matter, outside space and time, as Plato maintained. The bronze sphere derives its shape not from an ideal Sphere but from its maker, who introduces form into the appropriate matter in the process of his work. Likewise, Socrates' humanity derives not from an ideal Human but from his parents, who introduce form into the appropriate matter when they conceive him.

Thus, Aristotle reverses the question asked by Plato: "What is it that two human beings have in common that makes them both human?" He asks instead, "What makes two human beings two humans rather than one?" And his answer is that what makes Socrates distinct from his friend Callias is not their substantial form, which is the same, nor their accidental forms, which may be the same or different, but their matter. Matter, not form, is the principle of individuation.

CAUSATION

In several places Aristotle distinguishes four types of cause, or explanation. First, he says, there is that of which and out of which a thing is made, such as the bronze of a statue. This is called the material cause. Second, there is the form or pattern of a thing, which may be expressed in its definition; Aristotle's example is the proportion of the length of two strings in a lyre, which is the formal cause of one note's being the octave of another. The third type of cause is the origin of a change or state of rest in something; this is often called the "efficient cause." Aristotle gives as examples a person reaching a decision, a father begetting a child, a sculptor carving a statue, and a doctor healing a patient. The fourth and last type of cause is the end or goal of a thing—that for the sake of which a thing is done. This is known as the "final cause."

Although Aristotle gives mathematical examples of formal causes, the forms whose causation interests him most are the substantial forms of living beings. In these cases substantial form is the structure or organization of the being as a whole, as well as of its various parts; it is this structure that explains the being's life cycle and characteristic activities. In these cases, in fact, formal and final causes coincide, the mature realization of natural form being the end to which the activities of the organism tend. The growth and development of the various parts of a living being, such as the root of a tree or the heart of a sheep, can be understood only as the actualization of a certain structure for the purpose of performing a certain biological function.

BEING

For Aristotle, "being" is whatever *is* anything whatever. Whenever Aristotle explains the meaning of *being*, he does so by explaining the sense of the Greek verb *to be*. Being contains whatever items can be the subjects of true propositions containing the word *is*, whether or not the *is* is followed by a predicate. Thus, both *Socrates is* and *Socrates is wise* say something about being. Every being in any category other than substance is a property or a modification of substance. For this reason, Aristotle says that the study of substance is the way to understand the nature of being. The books of the *Metaphysics* in which he undertakes this investigation, VII through IX, are among the most difficult of his writings.

Aristotle gives two superficially conflicting accounts of the subject matter of first philosophy. According to one account, it is the discipline "which theorizes about being qua being, and the things which belong to being taken in itself"; unlike the special sciences, it deals with the most general features of beings, insofar as they are beings. On the other account, first philosophy deals with a particular kind of being, namely, divine, independent, and immutable substance; for this reason he sometimes calls the discipline "theology."

It is important to note that these accounts are not simply two different descriptions of "being qua being." There is, indeed, no such thing as being qua being; there are only different ways of studying being. When one studies human physiology, for example, one studies humans qua animals—that is to say, one studies the structures and functions that humans have in common with animals. But of course there is no such entity as a "human qua animal." Similarly, to study something as a being is to study it in virtue of what it has in common with all other things. To study the universe as being is to study it as a single overarching system, embracing all the causes of things coming into being and remaining in existence.

THE UNMOVED MOVER

The way in which Aristotle seeks to show that the universe is a single causal system is through an examination of the notion of movement, which finds its culmination in Book XI of the *Metaphysics*. As noted above, *motion*, for

Aristotle, refers to change in any of several different categories. Aristotle's fundamental principle is that everything that is in motion is moved by something else, and he offers a number of (unconvincing) arguments to this effect. He then argues that there cannot be an infinite series of moved movers. If it is true that when A is in motion there must be some B that moves A, then if B is itself in motion there must be some C moving B, and so on. This series cannot go on forever, and so it must come to a halt in some X that is a cause of motion but does not move itself—an unmoved mover.

Since the motion it causes is everlasting, this X must itself be an eternal substance. It must lack matter, for it cannot come into existence or go out of existence by turning into anything else. It must also lack potentiality, for the mere power to cause motion would not ensure the sempiternity of motion. It must, therefore, be pure actuality (*energeia*). Although the revolving heavens, for Aristotle, lack the possibility of substantial change, they possess potentiality, because each heavenly body has the power to move elsewhere in its diurnal round. Since these bodies are in motion, they need a mover, and this is a motionless mover. Such a mover could not act as an efficient cause, because that would involve a change in itself, but it can act as a final cause—an object of love—because being loved does not involve any change in the beloved. The stars and planets seek to imitate the perfection of the unmoved mover by moving about the Earth in a circle, the most perfect of shapes. For this to be the case, of course, the heavenly bodies must have souls capable of feeling love for the unmoved mover. "On such a principle," Aristotle says, "depend the heavens and the world of nature."

Aristotle is prepared to call the unmoved mover "God." The life of God, he says, must be like the very best of human lives. The delight that a human being takes in the sublimest moments of philosophical contemplation is in God a perpetual state. What, Aristotle asks, does God think of? He must think of something—otherwise, he is no better than a sleeping human—and whatever he is thinking of, he must think of eternally. Either he thinks about himself, or he thinks about something else. But the value of a thought depends on the value of what it is a thought of, so, if God were thinking of anything other than himself, he would be somehow degraded. So he must be thinking of himself, the supreme being, and his life is a thinking of thinking (*noesis noeseos*).

This conclusion has been much debated. Some have regarded it as a sublime truth; others have thought it a piece of exquisite nonsense. Among those who have taken the latter view, some have considered it the supreme absurdity of Aristotle's system, and others have held that Aristotle himself intended it as a reductio ad absurdum. Whatever the truth about the object of thought of the unmoved mover, it seems clear that it does not include the contingent affairs of individual human beings.

Thus, at the supreme point of Aristotle's causal hierarchy stand the heavenly movers, moved and unmoved, which are the final cause of all generation and corruption. And this is why metaphysics can be called by two such different names. When Aristotle says that first philosophy studies the whole of being, he is describing it by indicating the field it is to explain; when he says that it is the science of the divine, he is describing it by indicating its ultimate principles of explanation. Thus, first philosophy is both the science of being qua being and also theology.

PHILOSOPHY OF MIND

Aristotle regarded psychology as a part of natural philosophy, and he wrote much about the philosophy of mind.

This material appears in his ethical writings, in a systematic treatise on the nature of the soul (*De anima*), and in a number of minor monographs on topics such as sense-perception, memory, sleep, and dreams.

For Aristotle the biologist, the soul is not—as it was in some of Plato's writings—an exile from a better world ill-housed in a base body. The soul's very essence is defined by its relationship to an organic structure. Not only humans but beasts and plants too have souls, intrinsic principles of animal and vegetable life. A soul, Aristotle says, is "the actuality of a body that has life," where life means the capacity for self-sustenance, growth, and reproduction. If one regards a living substance as a composite of matter and form, then the soul is the form of a natural—or, as Aristotle sometimes says, organic—body. An organic body is a body that has organs—that is to say, parts that have specific functions, such as the mouths of mammals and the roots of trees.

The souls of living beings are ordered by Aristotle in a hierarchy. Plants have a vegetative or nutritive soul, which consists of the powers of growth, nutrition, and reproduction. Animals have, in addition, the powers of perception and locomotion—they possess a sensitive soul, and every animal has at least one sense-faculty, touch being the most universal. Whatever can feel at all can feel pleasure; hence, animals, which have senses, also have desires. Humans, in addition, have the power of reason and thought (*logismos kai dianoia*), which may be called a rational soul. The way in which Aristotle structured the soul and its faculties influenced not only philosophy but also science for nearly two millennia.

Aristotle's theoretical concept of soul differs from that of Plato before him and René Descartes (1596–1650) after him. A soul, for him, is not an interior immaterial agent acting on a body. Soul and body are no more distinct from each other than the impress of a seal is distinct from the wax on which it is impressed. The parts of the soul, moreover, are faculties, which are distinguished from each other by their operations and their objects. The power of growth is distinct from the power of sensation because growing and feeling are two different activities, and the sense of sight differs from the sense of hearing not because eyes are different from ears but because colours are different from sounds.

The objects of sense come in two kinds: those that are proper to particular senses, such as colour, sound, taste, and smell, and those that are perceptible by more than one sense, such as motion, number, shape, and size. One can tell, for example, whether something is moving either by watching it or by feeling it, and so motion is a "common sensible." Although there is no special organ for detecting common sensibles, there is a faculty that Aristotle calls a "central sense." When one encounters a horse, for example, one may see, hear, feel, and smell it; it is the central sense that unifies these sensations into perceptions of a single object (though the knowledge that this object is a horse is, for Aristotle, a function of intellect rather than sense).

Besides the five senses and the central sense, Aristotle recognizes other faculties that later came to be grouped together as the "inner senses," notably imagination and memory. Even at the purely philosophical level, however, Aristotle's accounts of the inner senses are unrewarding.

At the same level within the hierarchy as the senses, which are cognitive faculties, there is also an affective faculty, which is the locus of spontaneous feeling. This is a part of the soul that is basically irrational but is capable of being controlled by reason. It is the locus of desire and passion; when brought under the sway of reason, it is the seat of the moral virtues, such as courage and temperance. The highest level of the soul is occupied by mind or reason, the locus of thought and understanding. Thought differs from sense-perception and is the prerogative, on earth, of human beings. Thought, like sensation, is a matter of making judgments; but sensation concerns particulars, while intellectual knowledge is of universals. Reasoning may be practical or theoretical, and, accordingly, Aristotle distinguishes between a deliberative and a speculative faculty.

In a notoriously difficult passage of *De anima*, Aristotle introduces a further distinction between two kinds of mind: one passive, which can "become all things," and one active, which can "make all things." The active mind, he says, is "separable, impassible, and unmixed." In antiquity and the Middle Ages, this passage was the subject of sharply different interpretations. Some—particularly among Arab commentators—identified the separable active agent with God or with some other superhuman intelligence. Others—particularly among Latin commentators—took Aristotle to be identifying two different faculties within the human mind: an active intellect, which formed concepts, and a passive intellect, which was a storehouse of ideas and beliefs.

If the second interpretation is correct, then Aristotle is here recognizing a part of the human soul that is separable from the body and immortal. Here and elsewhere there is detectable in Aristotle, in addition to his standard biological notion of the soul, a residue of a Platonic vision according to which the intellect is a distinct entity separable from the body. No one has produced a wholly satisfactory reconciliation between the biological and the transcendent strains in Aristotle's thought.

ETHICS

The surviving works of Aristotle include three treatises on moral philosophy: the *Nicomachean Ethics* in 10 books, the *Eudemian Ethics* in 7 books, and the *Magna moralia* (Latin: "Great Ethics"). The *Nicomachean Ethics* is generally regarded as the most important of the three; it consists of a series of short treatises, possibly brought together by Aristotle's son Nicomachus. In the 19th century the *Eudemian Ethics* was often suspected of being the work of Aristotle's pupil Eudemus of Rhodes, but there is no good reason to doubt its authenticity. Interestingly, the *Nicomachean Ethics* and the *Eudemian Ethics* have three books in common: books V, VI, and VII of the former are the same as books IV, V, and VI of the latter. Although the question has been disputed for centuries, it is most likely that the original home of the common books was the *Eudemian Ethics*; it is also probable that Aristotle used this work for a course on ethics that he taught at the Lyceum during his mature period. The *Magna moralia* probably consists of notes taken by an unknown student of such a course.

HAPPINESS

Aristotle's approach to ethics is teleological. If life is to be worth living, he argues, it must surely be for the sake of something that is an end in itself—i.e., desirable for its own sake. If there is any single thing that is the highest human good, therefore, it must be desirable for its own sake, and all other goods must be desirable for the sake of it. Traditional Greek conceptions of the good life included the life of prosperity and the life of social position, in which case virtue would be the possession of wealth or nobility (and perhaps physical beauty). The overwhelming tendency of ancient philosophy, however, was to conceive of the good life as something that is the accomplishment of an individual—something that an individual does or does not do for himself. Moreover, once won, it is hard to take away.

As Aristotle explains in both the *Nichomachean Ethics* and the *Eudemian Ethics*, one popular conception of the highest human good is pleasure—the sensual pleasures of food, drink, and sex, combined with pleasures of the mind, including aesthetic and intellectual pleasures. Other people prefer a life of virtuous action in the political sphere (the quintessential example of this kind of life is Pericles [*c.* 495–429 BCE], the Athenian statesman who was largely responsible for the full development of Athenian democracy and the Athenian empire in the 5th century BCE). A third possible candidate for the highest human good is scientific or philosophical contemplation; an outstanding example of this kind of life is that of Aristotle himself. Aristotle thus reduces the answers to the question "What is a good life?" to a short list of three: the philosophical life, the political life, and the voluptuary life. This triad provides the key to his ethical inquiry.

"Happiness," the term that Aristotle uses to designate the highest human good, is the usual translation of the ancient Greek *eudaimonia*. Although it is impossible to abandon the English term at this stage of history, it should be borne in mind that what Aristotle means by *eudaimonia* is something more like well-being or flourishing than any feeling of contentment. (The ancient Greek word *eudaimonia* means literally "the state of having a good indwelling spirit, a good genius"; thus "happiness" is not at all an adequate translation of this word.) Aristotle argues, in fact, that happiness is activity of the rational soul in accordance with virtue. Thus, the notions of happiness and virtue are linked.

According to Aristotle, human beings must have a function, because particular types of humans (e.g., sculptors) do, as do the parts and organs of individual human beings. This function must be unique to humans; thus, it cannot consist of growth and nourishment, for this is shared by plants, or the life of the senses, for this is shared by animals. It must therefore involve the peculiarly human faculty of reason. The highest human good is the same as good human functioning, and good human functioning is the same as the good exercise of the faculty of reason—that is to say, the activity of rational soul in accordance with virtue. There are two kinds of virtue: moral and intellectual. Moral virtues are exemplified by courage, temperance, and liberality; the key intellectual virtues are wisdom, which governs ethical behaviour, and understanding, which is expressed in scientific endeavour and contemplation.

VIRTUE

People's virtues are a subset of their good qualities. They are not innate, like eyesight, but are acquired by practice and lost by disuse. They are abiding states, and they thus differ from momentary passions such as anger and pity. Virtues are states of character that find expression both in purpose and in action. Moral virtue is expressed in good purpose—that is to say, in prescriptions for action in accordance with a good plan of life. It is expressed also in actions that avoid both excess and defect. A temperate person, for example, will avoid eating or drinking too much, but he will also avoid eating or drinking too little. Virtue chooses the mean, or middle ground, between excess and defect. Besides purpose and action, virtue is also concerned with feeling. One may, for example, be excessively concerned with sex or insufficiently interested in it; the temperate person will take the appropriate degree of interest and be neither lustful nor frigid.

While all the moral virtues are means of action and passion, it is not the case that every kind of action and passion is capable of a virtuous mean. There are some actions of which there is no right amount, because any amount of them is too much; Aristotle gives murder and adultery as examples. The virtues, besides being concerned with means of action and passion, are themselves means in the sense that they occupy a middle ground between two contrary vices. Thus, the virtue of courage is flanked on one side by foolhardiness and on the other by cowardice.

Aristotle's account of virtue as a mean is no truism. It is a distinctive ethical theory that contrasts with other influential systems of various kinds. It contrasts, on the one hand, with religious systems that give a central role to the concept of a moral law, concentrating on the prohibitive aspects of morality. It also differs from moral systems such as utilitarianism that judge the rightness and wrongness of actions in terms of their consequences. Unlike the utilitarian, Aristotle believes that there are some kinds of action that are morally wrong in principle.

The mean that is the mark of moral virtue is determined by the intellectual virtue of wisdom. Wisdom is characteristically expressed in the formulation of prescriptions for action—"practical syllogisms," as Aristotle calls them. A practical syllogism consists of a general recipe for a good life, followed by an accurate description of the agent's actual circumstances and concluding with a decision about the appropriate action to be carried out.

Wisdom, the intellectual virtue that is proper to practical reason, is inseparably linked with the moral virtues of the affective part of the soul. Only if an agent possesses moral virtue will he endorse an appropriate recipe for a good life. Only if he is gifted with intelligence will he make an accurate assessment of the circumstances in which his decision is to be made. It is impossible, Aristotle says, to be really good without wisdom or to be really wise without moral virtue. Only when correct reasoning and right desire come together does truly virtuous action result.

Virtuous action, then, is always the result of successful practical reasoning. But practical reasoning may be defective in various ways. Someone may operate from a vicious choice of lifestyle; a glutton, for example, may plan his life around the project of always maximizing the present pleasure. Aristotle calls such a person "intemperate." Even people who do not endorse such a hedonistic premise may, once in a while, overindulge. This failure to apply to a particular occasion a generally sound plan of life Aristotle calls "incontinence."

ACTION AND CONTEMPLATION

The pleasures that are the domain of temperance, intemperance, and incontinence are the familiar bodily pleasures of food, drink, and sex. In his treatment of pleasure, however, Aristotle explores a much wider field. There are two classes of aesthetic pleasures: the pleasures of the inferior senses of touch and taste, and the pleasures of the superior senses of sight, hearing, and smell. Finally, at the top of the scale, there are the pleasures of the mind.

Plato had posed the question of whether the best life consists in the pursuit of pleasure or the exercise of the intellectual virtues. Aristotle's answer is that, properly understood, the two are not in competition with each other. The exercise of the highest form of virtue is the very same thing as the truest form of pleasure; each is identical with the other and with happiness. The highest virtues are the intellectual ones, and among them Aristotle distinguished between wisdom and understanding. To the question of whether happiness is to be identified with the pleasure of wisdom or with the pleasure of understanding, Aristotle gives different answers in his main ethical treatises. In the *Nicomachean Ethics* perfect happiness, though it presupposes the moral virtues, is constituted solely by the activity of philosophical contemplation, whereas in the *Eudemian Ethics* it consists in the harmonious exercise of all the virtues, intellectual and moral.

The Eudemian ideal of happiness, given the role it assigns to contemplation, to the moral virtues, and to pleasure, can claim to combine the features of the traditional three lives—the life of the philosopher, the life of the politician, and the life of the pleasure seeker. The happy person will value contemplation above all, but part of his happy life will consist in the exercise of moral virtues in the political sphere and the enjoyment in moderation of the natural human pleasures of body as well as of soul. But even in the *Eudemian Ethics* it is "the service and contemplation of God" that sets the standard for the appropriate exercise of the moral virtues, and in the *Nicomachean Ethics* this contemplation is described as a superhuman activity of a divine part of human nature. Aristotle's final word on ethics is that, despite being mortal, human beings must strive to make themselves immortal as far as they can.

POLITICAL THEORY

Turning from the *Ethics* treatises to their sequel, the *Politics*, the reader is brought down to earth. "Man is a political animal," Aristotle observes; human beings are creatures of flesh and blood, rubbing shoulders with each other in cities and communities. Like his work in zoology, Aristotle's political studies combine observation and theory. He and his students documented the constitutions of 158 states—one of which, *The Constitution of Athens*, has survived on papyrus. The aim of the *Politics*, Aristotle says, is to investigate, on the basis of the constitutions collected, what makes for good government and what makes for bad government and to identify the factors favourable or unfavourable to the preservation of a constitution.

Aristotle asserts that all communities aim at some good. The state (*polis*), by which he means a city-state such as Athens, is the highest kind of community, aiming at the highest of goods. The most primitive communities are families of men and women, masters and slaves. Families combine to make a village, and several villages combine to make a state, which is the first self-sufficient community. The state is no less natural than the family; this is proved by the fact that human beings have the power of speech, the purpose of which is "to set forth the expedient and inexpedient, and therefore likewise the just and the unjust." The foundation of the state was the greatest of benefactions, because only within a state can human beings fulfill their potential.

This map shows some of the major city-states of Greece in the 4th century BCE. Aristotle believed the city-state to be the highest form of community. Courtesy of the University of Texas Libraries, The University of Texas at Austin

Government, Aristotle says, must be in the hands of one, of a few, or of the many; and governments may govern for the general good or for the good of the rulers. Government by a single person for the general good is called "monarchy"; for private benefit, "tyranny." Government by a minority is "aristocracy" if it aims at the state's best interest and "oligarchy" if it benefits only the ruling minority. Popular government in the common interest Aristotle calls "polity"; he reserves the word "democracy" for anarchic mob rule.

If a community contains an individual or family of outstanding excellence, then, Aristotle says, monarchy is the best constitution. But such a case is very rare, and the risk of miscarriage is great, for monarchy corrupts into tyranny, which is the worst constitution of all. Aristocracy, in theory, is the next-best constitution after monarchy (because the ruling minority will be the best-qualified to rule), but in practice Aristotle preferred a kind of constitutional democracy, for what he called "polity" is a state in which rich and poor respect each other's rights and the best-qualified citizens rule with the consent of all.

Two elements of Aristotle's teaching affected European political institutions for many centuries: his justification of slavery and his condemnation of usury. Some people, Aristotle says, think that the rule of master over slave is contrary to nature and therefore unjust. But they are quite wrong: a slave is someone who is by nature not his own property but someone else's. Aristotle agrees, however, that in practice much slavery is unjust, and he speculates that, if nonliving machines could be made to carry out menial tasks, there would be no need for slaves as living tools. Nevertheless, some people are so inferior and brutish that it is better for them to be controlled by a master than to be left to their own devices.

Although not himself an aristocrat, Aristotle had an aristocratic disdain for commerce. Our possessions, he says, have two uses, proper and improper. Money too has a proper and an improper use; its proper use is to be exchanged for goods and services, not to be lent out at interest. Of all the methods of making money, "taking a breed from barren metal" is the most unnatural.

RHETORIC AND POETICS

Rhetoric, for Aristotle, is a topic-neutral discipline that studies the possible means of persuasion. In advising orators on how to exploit the moods of their audience, Aristotle undertakes a systematic and often insightful treatment of human emotion, dealing in turn with anger, hatred, fear, shame, pity, indignation, envy, and jealousy— in each case offering a definition of the emotion and a list of its objects and causes.

The *Poetics* is much better known than the *Rhetoric*, though only the first book of the former, a treatment of epic and tragic poetry, survives. The book aims, among other things, to answer Plato's criticisms of representative art. According to the theory of Forms, material objects are imperfect copies of original, real, Forms; artistic representations of material objects are therefore only copies of copies, at two removes from reality. Moreover, drama has a specially corrupting effect, because it stimulates unworthy emotions in its audience. In response, Aristotle insists that imitation, so far from being the degrading activity that Plato describes, is something natural to humans from childhood and is one of the characteristics that makes humans superior to animals, since it vastly increases the scope of what they may learn.

In order to answer Plato's complaint that playwrights are only imitators of everyday life, which is itself only an imitation of the real world of Forms, Aristotle draws a contrast between poetry and history. The poet's job is to describe not something that has actually happened but something that might well happen—that is to say, something that is possible because it is necessary or likely. For this reason, poetry is more philosophical and more important than history, for poetry speaks of the universal, history of only the particular. Much of what happens to people in everyday life is a matter of sheer accident; only in fiction can one witness character and action work themselves out to their natural consequences.

Far from debasing the emotions, as Plato thought, drama has a beneficial effect on them. Tragedy, Aristotle says, must contain episodes arousing pity and fear so as to achieve a "purification" of these emotions. No one is quite sure exactly what Aristotle meant by *katharsis*, or purification. But perhaps what he meant was that watching tragedy helps people to put their own sorrows and worries in perspective, because in it they observe how catastrophe can overtake even people who are vastly their superiors.

THE LEGACY OF ARISTOTLE

Since the Renaissance it has been traditional to regard the Academy and the Lyceum as two opposite poles of philosophy. Plato is idealistic, utopian, otherworldly; Aristotle is realistic, utilitarian, commonsensical. In fact, however, the doctrines that Plato and Aristotle share are more important than those that divide them. Many post-Renaissance historians of ideas have been less perceptive than the commentators of late antiquity, who saw it as their duty to construct a harmonious concord between the two greatest philosophers of the known world.

By any reckoning, Aristotle's intellectual achievement is stupendous. He was the first genuine scientist in history.

He was the first author whose surviving works contain detailed and extensive observations of natural phenomena, and he was the first philosopher to achieve a sound grasp of the relationship between observation and theory in scientific method. He identified the various scientific disciplines and explored their relationships to each other. He was the first professor to organize his lectures into courses and to assign them a place in a syllabus. His Lyceum was the first research institute in which a number of scholars and investigators joined in collaborative inquiry and documentation. Finally, and not least important, he was the first person in history to build up a research library, a systematic collection of works to be used by his colleagues and to be handed on to posterity.

Millennia later, Plato and Aristotle still have a strong claim to being the greatest philosophers who have ever lived. But if their contribution to philosophy is equal, it was Aristotle who made the greater contribution to the intellectual patrimony of the world. Not only every philosopher but also every scientist is in his debt. He deserves the title Dante gave him: "the master of those who know."

CHAPTER 5

HELLENISTIC AND ROMAN PHILOSOPHY

The period after the death of Aristotle was characterized by the decay of the Greek city-states, which then became pawns in the power game of the Hellenistic kings who succeeded Alexander. Life became troubled and insecure. It was in this environment that two dogmatic philosophical systems came into being, Stoicism and Epicureanism, which promised to give their adherents something to hold onto and to make them independent of the external world. Other schools that emerged or continued during the Hellenistic and late Roman periods were skepticism, Neo-Pythagoreanism, and Neoplatonism.

STOICISM

Stoicism was one of the loftiest and most sublime philosophies in the record of Western civilization. In urging participation in human affairs, Stoics believed that the goal of all inquiry is to provide the individual with a mode of conduct characterized by tranquillity of mind and certainty of moral worth.

THE NATURE AND SCOPE OF STOICISM

For the early Stoic philosopher, as for all the post-Aristotelian schools, knowledge and its pursuit are no longer held to be ends in themselves. The Hellenistic Age was a time of transition, and the Stoic philosopher was perhaps its most influential spokesperson. A new culture was in the making. The heritage of an earlier period, with Athens as its intellectual leader, was to continue, but to undergo many changes. If, as with Socrates, to know is to know oneself, rationality as the sole means by which something outside the self might be achieved may be said to be the hallmark of Stoic belief. As a Hellenistic philosophy, Stoicism presented an *ars vitae,* a way of accommodation for people to whom the human condition no longer appeared as the mirror of a universal, calm, and ordered existence. Reason alone could reveal the constancy of cosmic order and the originative source of unyielding value; thus, reason became the true model for human existence. To the Stoic, virtue is an inherent feature of the world, no less inexorable in relation to humanity than are the laws of nature.

The Stoics believed that perception is the basis of true knowledge. In logic, their comprehensive presentation of the topic is derived from perception, yielding not only the judgment that knowledge is possible but also the judgment that it is possible to have knowledge that is absolutely certain. To them, the world is composed of material things, with some few exceptions (e.g., meaning), and the irreducible element in all things is right reason, which pervades the world as divine fire. Things, such as material, or corporeal, bodies, are governed by this reason or fate, in which virtue is inherent. The world in its awesome entirety is so ruled as to exhibit a grandeur of orderly arrangement that can only serve as a standard for humans in the regulation and ordering of their lives. Thus, the goal of humanity is to live according to nature, in agreement with the world design. Stoic moral theory is also based on the view that the world, as one great city, is a unity. The human individual, as a world citizen, has an obligation and loyalty to all things in that city. He or she must play an active role in world affairs, remembering that the world exemplifies virtue and right action. Thus, moral worth, duty, and justice are singularly Stoic emphases, together with a certain sternness of mind. For the moral human neither is merciful nor shows pity, because each suggests a deviation from duty and from the fated necessity that rules the world. Nonetheless—with its loftiness of spirit and its emphasis on the essential worth of all humans—the themes of universal brotherhood and the benevolence of divine nature make Stoicism one of the most appealing of philosophies.

EARLY GREEK STOICISM

With the death of Aristotle (322 BCE) and that of Alexander the Great (323 BCE), the greatness of the life and thought of the Greek city-state (polis) ended. With Athens no longer the centre of worldly attraction, its claim to urbanity and cultural prominence passed on to other cities—to Rome, to Alexandria, and to Pergamum. The Greek polis gave way to larger political units; local rule was replaced by that of distant governors. The earlier distinction between Greek and barbarian was destroyed; provincial and tribal loyalties were broken apart, first by Alexander and then by Roman legions. The loss of freedom by subject peoples further encouraged a deterioration of the concept of the freeman and resulted in the rendering of obligation and service to a ruler whose moral force held little meaning. The earlier intimacy of order, cosmic and civic, was now replaced by social and political disorder; and traditional mores gave way to uncertain and transient values.

Stoicism had its beginnings in a changing world, in which earlier codes of conduct and ways of understanding proved no longer suitable. But it was also influenced by tenets of the older schools. Of the several schools of philosophy stemming from Socrates, the Cynic and Megarian schools were influential in the early development of Stoic doctrine: the Cynics for their emphasis on the simple life, unadorned and free of emotional involvement; and the Megarians for their study of dialectic, logical form, and paradoxes.

Stoicism takes its name from the place where its founder, Zeno of Citium (Cyprus), customarily lectured— the Stoa Poikile (Painted Colonnade). Zeno, who flourished in the early 3rd century BCE, showed in his own doctrines the influence of earlier Greek attitudes, particularly those mentioned above. He was apparently well versed in Platonic thought, for he had studied at Plato's Academy both with Xenocrates of Chalcedon and with Polemon of Athens, successive heads of the Academy. Zeno was responsible for the division of philosophy into three parts: logic, physics, and ethics. He also established the central Stoic doctrines in each part, so that later Stoics were to expand rather than to change radically the views of the founder. With some exceptions (in the field of logic), Zeno thus provided the following themes as the essential framework of Stoic philosophy: logic as an

A bust of Zeno of Citium, the father of Stoicism. Museo Capitolino, Rome, Italy/The Bridgeman Art Library/ Getty Images

instrument and not as an end in itself; human happiness as a product of life according to nature; physical theory as providing the means by which right actions are to be determined; perception as the basis of certain knowledge; the wise person as the model of human excellence; Platonic forms as being unreal; true knowledge as always accompanied by assent; the fundamental substance of all existing things as being a divine fire, the universal principles of which are (1) passive (matter) and (2) active (reason inherent in matter); belief in a world conflagration and renewal; belief in the corporeality of all things; belief in the fated causality that necessarily binds all things; cosmopolitanism, or cultural outlook transcending narrower loyalties; and the individual's obligation, or duty, to choose only those acts that are in accord with nature, all other acts being a matter of indifference.

Cleanthes of Assos, who succeeded Zeno as head of the school, is best known for his *Hymn to Zeus,* which movingly describes Stoic reverence for the cosmic order and the power of universal reason and law. The third head of the school, Chrysippus of Soli, who lived to the end of the 3rd century, was perhaps the greatest and certainly the most productive of the early Stoics. He devoted his considerable energies to the almost complete development of the Zenonian themes in logic, physics, and ethics. In logic particularly, he defended against the Megarian logicians and the skeptics such concepts as certain knowledge, comprehensive presentation, proposition and argument, truth and its criterion, and assent. His work in propositional logic, in which unanalyzed propositions joined by connectives are studied, made important contributions to the history of ancient logic and is of particular relevance to more recent developments in logic.

In physics, Chrysippus was responsible for the attempt to show that fate and free will are not mutually exclusive conceptual features of Stoic doctrine. He further distinguished between "whole" and "all," or "universe," arguing that the whole is the world, while the all is the external void together with the world. Zeno's view of the origin of human beings as providentially generated by "fiery reason" out of matter was expanded by Chrysippus to include the concept of self-preservation, which governs all living things. Another earlier view (Zeno's), that of nature as a model for life, was amplified first by Cleanthes and then by Chrysippus. The Zenonian appeal to life "according to nature" had evidently been left vague, because to Cleanthes it seemed necessary to speak of life in accord with nature conceived as the world at large (the cosmos), whereas Chrysippus distinguished between world nature and human nature. Thus, to do good is to act in accord with both human and universal nature. Chrysippus also expanded the Stoic view that seminal reasons were the impetus for animate motion.

He established firmly that logic and (especially) physics are necessary and are means for the differentiation of goods and evils. Thus, a knowledge of physics (or theology) is required before an ethics can be formulated. Indeed, physics and logic find their value chiefly in this very purpose. Chrysippus covered almost every feature of Stoic doctrine and treated each so thoroughly that the essential features of the school were to change relatively little after his time.

LATER ROMAN STOICISM

The Middle Stoa, which flourished in the 2nd and early 1st centuries BCE, was dominated chiefly by two men of Rhodes: Panaetius, its founder, and his disciple Poseidonius. Panaetius organized a Stoic school in Rome before returning to Athens, and Poseidonius was largely responsible for an emphasis on the religious features of the doctrine. Both were antagonistic to the ethical doctrines of Chrysippus, who, they believed, had strayed too far from the Platonic and Aristotelian roots of Stoicism. It may have been because of the considerable time that Panaetius and Poseidonius lived in Rome that the Stoa there turned so much of its emphasis to the moral and religious themes within the Stoic doctrine. Panaetius was highly regarded by Cicero, who used him as a model for his own work. Poseidonius, who had been a disciple of Panaetius in Athens, taught Cicero at his school at Rhodes and later went to Rome and remained there for a time with Cicero. If Poseidonius admired Plato and Aristotle, he was particularly interested—unlike most of his school—in the study of natural and providential phenomena. In presenting the Stoic system in the second book of *De natura deorum* (45 BCE), Cicero most probably followed Poseidonius. Because his master, Panaetius, was chiefly concerned with concepts of duty and obligation, it was his studies that served as a model for the *De officiis* (44 BCE) of Cicero. Hecaton, another of Panaetius' students and an active Stoic philosopher, also stressed similar ethical themes.

If Chrysippus is to be commended for his diligence in defending Stoic logic and epistemology against the skepticism of the New Academy (3rd–2nd century BCE), it was chiefly Panaetius and Poseidonius who were responsible for the widespread popularity of Stoicism in Rome. It was precisely their turning of doctrine to themes in moral philosophy and natural science that appealed to the intensely practical Romans. The times perhaps demanded such interests, and with them Stoicism was to become predominantly a philosophy for the individual, showing how—given the vicissitudes of life—one might be stoical. Law, world citizenship, nature, and the benevolent workings of Providence and the divine reason were the principal areas of interest of Stoicism at this time.

These tendencies toward practicality are also well illustrated in the later period of the school (in the first two centuries CE) in the writings of Lucius Seneca, a Roman statesman; of Epictetus, a slave freed by the Roman emperor Nero; and of Marcus Aurelius, an emperor of the 2nd century CE. Both style and content in the *Libri morales* (*Moral Essays*) and *Epistulae morales* (*Moral Letters*) of Seneca reinforce the new direction in Stoic thought. The *Encheiridion* (*Manual*) of Epictetus and the *Meditations* of Marcus Aurelius furthered the sublime and yet personal consolation of the Stoic message and increasingly showed the strength of its rivalry to the burgeoning power of the new Christianity. The mark of a guide, of the religious teacher, is preeminent in these writings. It is difficult to establish with any precision, however, the extent of Stoic influence by the time of the first half of the 2nd century CE. So popular had these ideas become that many specifically Stoic terms (viz., right reason, comprehension, assent, indifference, Logos, natural law, and the notion of the wise person) commonly were used in debate and intellectual disputes.

Bronze equestrian statue of Marcus Aurelius, in the Piazza del Campidoglio, Rome, c. 173 CE. Height 5.03 m. Alinari—Art Resource/EB Inc.

EPICUREANISM

The thought of Zeno's contemporary Epicurus (341–270 BCE) also constituted a philosophy of defense in a troubled world. In a strict sense, Epicureanism is simply the philosophy taught by Epicurus; in a broad sense, it is a system of ethics embracing every conception or form of life that can be traced to the principles of his philosophy. In ancient polemics, as often since, the term was employed with an even more generic (and clearly erroneous) meaning as the equivalent of hedonism, the doctrine that pleasure or happiness is the chief good. In popular parlance, Epicureanism thus means devotion to pleasure, comfort, and high living, with a certain nicety of style.

THE NATURE OF EPICUREANISM

Several fundamental concepts characterize the philosophy of Epicurus. In physics, these are atomism, a mechanical conception of causality—limited, however, by the idea of a spontaneous motion, or "swerve," of the atoms, which interrupts the necessary effect of a cause—the infinity of the universe and the equilibrium of all forces that circularly enclose its phenomena; and the existence of gods conceived as beatified and immortal natures completely extraneous to happenings in the world. In ethics, the basic concepts are the identification of good with pleasure and of the supreme good and ultimate end with the absence of pain from the body and the soul—a limit beyond which pleasure does not grow but changes; the reduction of every human relation to the principle of utility, which finds its highest expression in friendship, in which it is at the same time surmounted; and, in accordance with this end, the limitation of all desire and the practice of the virtues, from which pleasure is inseparable, and a withdrawn and quiet life.

In principle, Epicurus' ethic of pleasure is the exact opposite of the Stoic's ethic of duty. The consequences, however, are the same: in the end, the Epicurean is forced to live with the same temperance and justice as the Stoic. Of utmost importance, however, is one point of divergence: the walls of the Stoic's city are those of the world, and its law is that of reason; the limits of the Epicurean's city are those of a garden, and the law is that of friendship. Although this garden can also reach the boundaries of earth, its centre is always a human individual.

THE WORKS AND DOCTRINE OF EPICURUS

Epicurus' predecessors were Leucippus and Democritus in physics and Antiphon Sophista, Aristippus of Cyrene, and Eudoxus of Cnidus (a geometer and astronomer) in ethics. Epicurus differed from all of these in his systematic spirit and in the unity that he tried to give to every part of philosophy. In this respect, he was greatly influenced by the philosophy and teachings of Aristotle — taking over the essentials of his doctrines and pursuing the problems that he posed. In 306 BCE, Epicurus established his school at Athens in his garden, from which it came to be known as The Garden.

In accordance with the goal that he assigned to philosophy, Epicurus' teaching had a dogmatic character, in substance if not in form. He called his treatises *dialogismoi,* or "conversations." Since the utility of the doctrines lay in their application, he summarized them in *stoicheia,* or "elementary propositions," to be memorized. The number of works produced by Epicurus and his disciples reveals an impressive theoretical activity. But no less important was the practical action in living by the virtues taught by him and in honouring the obligations of reciprocal help in the name of friendship. In these endeavours, continuous assistance was rendered by Epicurus himself, who, even when old and ill, was occupied in writing letters of admonishment, guidance, and comfort—everywhere announcing his gospel of peace and, under the name of pleasure, inviting to love.

Philosophy was, for Epicurus, the art of living, and it aimed at the same time both to assure happiness and to supply means to achieve it. As for science, Epicurus was concerned only with the practical end in view. If possible, he would have done without it. "If we were not troubled by our suspicions of the phenomena of the sky and about death," he wrote, "and also by our failure to grasp the lim-

its of pain and desires, we should have no need of natural science." But this science requires a principle that guarantees its possibilities and its certainty and a method of constructing it. This principle and this method are the object of the "Canon," which Epicurus substituted for Logic. Since he made the "Canon" an integral introduction to the "Physics," however, his philosophy falls into two parts, the "Physics" and the "Ethics."

Rendering of Epicurus. Hulton Archive/Getty Images

The name canon, which means "rule," is

derived from a special work entitled "On the Criterion, or Canon." It held that all sensations and representations are true and serve as criteria. The same holds for pleasure and pain, the basic feelings to which all others can be traced. Also true, and included among the criteria, are what may be called concepts (*prolēpsis*), which consist of "a recollection of what has often been presented from without." Humans, therefore, must always cling to that "which was originally thought" in relation to every single "term" and which constitutes its background. Since the truth attested by each of the criteria is reflected in the *phainomena,* humans must cling to these, employing them as "signs," and must "conjecture" whatever "does not appear." With the use of signs and conjecture, however, the level of judgment is reached, and thought is well advanced into that sphere in which error is possible, a state that begins as soon as single terms are tied into a proposition. Error, which consists of what "our judgment adds" to the evidence, can be of two types, one relative to what is not an object of experience, the other relative to what is such an object but for which the evidence is dubious. Each type has its own method of proof. Following the principles and methods of the "Canon," Epicurus arrived at an atomism that, like that of the ancient naturalist Democritus, taught that the atoms, the void-space in which they move, and the worlds are all infinite. But in contrast to Democritus, who had followed the deductive route of the intellect, considering the knowledge of the senses to be spurious, Epicurus, following an inductive route, assigned truth to sensation and reduced the intellect to it. On the basis of the totality of problems as Aristotle posed them in his *Physics,* Epicurus modified entirely the mechanical theory of causes and of motion found in Democritus and added the concept of a natural necessity, which he called nature, and that of free causality, which alone could explain the

freedom of motion of humans and animals. For this purpose he distinguished three forms of motion in the atoms:
a natural one of falling in a straight line, owing to their
weight; a forced one due to impacts; and a free motion of
declination, or swerving from a straight line. Secondly, he
made finite the number of forms of the atoms in order to
limit the number of sensible qualities, since each form
begets a distinctive quality, and he taught a mathematical
as well as a physical atomism. Lest an infinity of sensible
qualities be generated, however, by an infinity of aggrega-
tions (if not of atomic kinds), Epicurus developed, from
just this concept of infinity, the law of universal equilibrium of all the forces, or "isonomy." Upon it, enclosing the
events in a circle, he founded a theory of cyclic returns.

As part of his physics, Epicurus' psychology held that
the soul must be a body. It is made of very thin atoms of
four different species—motile, quiescent, igneous, and
ethereal—the last, thinnest and the most mobile of all,
serving to explain sensitivity and thought. Thus constituted, the soul is, from another perspective, bipartite: in
part distributed throughout the entire body and in part
collected in the chest. The first part is the locus of sensations and of the physical affects of pain and pleasure; the
second (entirely dissociated from the first) is the *psychē* par
excellence—the seat of thought, emotions, and will.
Thought is due not to the transmission of sense motion
but to the perception of images constituted by films that
continuously issue from all bodies and, retaining their
form, arrive at the *psychē* through the pores. The full autonomy and freedom of the *psychē* is assured, as, with an act of
apprehension, it seizes at every moment the images it
needs, meanwhile remaining master of its own feelings.

The object of ethics is to determine the end and the
means necessary to reach it. Taking his cue from experience, Epicurus looked to the animal kingdom for his

answer. He concluded from this cue that the chief end is pleasure. He distinguished two kinds—a "kinetic" pleasure of sense and a "static" pleasure, consisting in the absence of pain—and taught that the pleasure of sense is good, though it is not good merely as motion but rather as a motion favourable to the nature of the receiving sense organ. In essence, pleasure is the equilibrium of the being with itself, existing wherever there is no pain.

Epicurus concluded that "freedom from pain in the body and from trouble in the mind" is the ultimate aim of a happy life. The damages and the advantages following the realization of any desire must be measured in a calculus in which even pain must be faced with courage if the consequent pleasure will be of longer duration.

Having thus given order to life, however, the wise person must also provide him- or herself with security. This is achieved in two ways—by reducing his or her needs to a minimum and withdrawing, far from human competition and from the noise of the world, to "live hidden"; and by adding the private compact of friendship to the public compact from which laws arise. To be sure, friendship stems from utility; but, once born, it is desirable in itself. Epicurus then added that "for love of friendship one has even to put in jeopardy love itself"; for every existence, being alone, needs the other. "To eat and drink without a friend," he wrote, "is to devour like the lion and the wolf." Thus, the utility sublimates itself and changes into love. But as every love is intrepid, the wise man, "if his friend is put to torture, suffers as if he himself were there" and, if necessary, "will die for his friend." Thus, into the bloody world of his time, Epicurus could launch the cry: "Friendship runs dancing through the world bringing to us all the summons to wake and sing its praises."

If humans' unhappiness stemmed only from their own vain desires and from worldly dangers, this wisdom, founded upon prudence alone, would suffice. But besides these sources of unhappiness there are two great fears, fear of death and fear of the gods. If science, however, is effective in revealing the bounds of desire and (as already seen) in quelling the fear of the gods, it can also allay the fear of death. Regarding the soul as a body within another body, science envisions it as dissolving when the body dissolves. Death, then, "is nothing to us, so long as we exist, death is not with us; but when death comes, then we do not exist." But death is feared not only for what may be awaiting man in the beyond but also for itself. "I am not afraid of being dead," said the comic Epicharmus of Cos: "I just do not want to die." The very idea of not existing instills a fear that Epicurus considered to be the cause of all the passions that pain the soul and disorder people's lives. Against it Epicurus argued that if pleasure is perfect within each instant and "infinite time contains no greater pleasure than limited time, if one measures by reason the limits of pleasure," then all desire of immortality is vain. Thus, Epicurus' most distinguished pupil, Metrodorus of Lampsacus, could exclaim, *"bebiōtai"* ("I have lived"), and this would be quite enough. The person who has conquered the fear of death can also despise pain, which "if it is long lasting is light, and if it is intense is short" and brings death nearer. The wise person has only to replace the image of pain present in the flesh with that of blessings enjoyed, and he can be happy even "inside the bull of Phalaris." The most beautiful example was set by Epicurus at the moment of his death:

> *A happy day is this on which I write to you . . . The pains which I feel . . . could not be greater. But all of this is opposed by the happiness which the soul experiences, remembering our conversations of a bygone time.*

The ultimate concentration of all his wisdom is the *Tetrapharmacon,* preserved by Philodemus: "The gods are not to be feared. Death is not a thing that one must fear. Good is easy to obtain. Evil is easy to tolerate."

On account of its dogmatic character and its practical end, the philosophy of Epicurus was not subject to development, except in the polemic and in its application to themes that Epicurus either had treated briefly or had never dealt with at all. Epicurus' philosophy remained essentially unchanged. Once truth has been found, it requires no more discussion, particularly when it completely satisfies the end toward which human nature tends. The main thing is to see this end; all of the rest comes by itself, and there is no longer anything to do but follow Epicurus, "liberator" and "saviour," and to memorize his "oracular words."

SKEPTICISM

Skepticism, which was initiated by another of Zeno's contemporaries, Pyrrhon of Elis (*c.* 360–*c.* 272 BCE), was destined to become of great importance for the preservation of detailed knowledge of Hellenistic philosophy in general. Pyrrhon's importance for the history of philosophy lies in the fact that one of the later adherents of his doctrine, Sextus Empiricus (flourished 3rd century CE), wrote a large work, *Pros dogmatikous* ("Against the Dogmatists"), in which he tried to refute all of the philosophers who held positive views, and in so doing he quoted extensively from their works, thus preserving much that would otherwise have been lost.

In the West, skeptical philosophical attitudes began to appear in ancient Greece about the 5th century BCE. The Eleatic philosophers (those associated with the Greek city of Elea in Italy) rejected the existence of plurality and change, conceiving of reality as a static One, and they denied that reality could be described in terms of the categories of ordinary experience. On the other hand, Heracleitus and his pupil Cratylus thought that the world was in such a state of flux that no permanent, unchangeable truth about it could be found; and Xenophanes, a wandering poet and philosopher, doubted whether humans could distinguish true from false knowledge.

A more developed form of skepticism appeared in some of the views attributed to Socrates and in the views of certain Sophists. Socrates, as portrayed in the early dialogues of his pupil Plato, was always questioning the knowledge claims of others; in the *Apology*, he famously admits that all that he really knows is that he knows nothing. Socrates' enemy, the Sophist Protagoras, contended that "man is the measure of all things," a thesis that has been taken to imply a kind of skeptical relativism: no views are ultimately or objectively true, but each is merely one person's opinion. Another Sophist, Gorgias, advanced the skeptical-nihilist thesis that nothing exists; and, if something did exist, it could not be known; and, if it could be known, it could not be communicated.

The putative father of Greek skepticism, however, was Pyrrhon, who undertook the rare effort of trying to live his skepticism. He avoided committing himself to any views about what the world was really like and acted only according to appearances. In this way he sought happiness, or at least mental peace.

The first school of skeptical philosophy developed in the Academy, the school founded by Plato, in the 3rd century BCE and was thus called "Academic" skepticism. Starting from the skeptical doctrines of Socrates, its leaders, Arcesilaus and Carneades, set forth a series of epistemological arguments to show that nothing could be known, challenging primarily what were then the two foremost schools, Stoicism and Epicureanism. They denied that any criteria could be found for distinguishing the true from the false; instead, only reasonable or probable standards could be established. This limited, or probabilistic, skepticism was the view of the Academy until the 1st century BCE, when the Roman philosopher and orator Cicero was a student there. His *Academica* and *De natura deorum* are the main sources of modern knowledge of this movement. (St. Augustine's *Contra academicos*, composed some five centuries later, was intended as an answer to Cicero's views.)

The other major form of ancient skepticism was Pyrrhonism, apparently developed by medical skeptics in Alexandria. Beginning with Aenesidemus (1st century BCE), this movement, named after Pyrrhon, criticized the Academic skeptics because they claimed to know too much—namely, that nothing could be known and that some things are more probable than others. The Pyrrhonians advanced a series of tropes, or ways of opposing various kinds of knowledge claims, in order to bring about *epochē* (suspension of judgment). The Pyrrhonian attitude is preserved in the writings of one of its last leaders, Sextus Empiricus (2nd or 3rd century CE). In his *Outlines of Pyrrhonism* and *Adversus mathematicos,* Sextus presented the tropes developed by previous Pyrrhonists. The 10 tropes attributed to Aenesidemus showed the difficulties encountered by attempts to ascertain the truth or reliability of judgments based on sense information, owing to the variability and differences of human and animal perceptions. Other arguments raised difficulties in determining whether there are any reliable criteria or standards—logical, rational, or otherwise—for judging whether anything is true or false. To settle any disagreement, a criterion seems to be required. Any purported criterion, however, would have to be based either on another criterion—thus leading to an infinite regress of criteria—or on itself, which would be circular. Sextus offered arguments to challenge any claims of dogmatic philosophers to know more than what is evident, and in so doing he presented, in one form or another, practically all of the skeptical arguments that have ever appeared in subsequent philosophy.

Sextus said that his arguments were aimed at leading people to a state of *ataraxia* (unperturbability). People who thought that they could know reality were constantly disturbed and frustrated. If they could be led to suspend judgment, however, they would find peace of mind. In this state of suspension they would neither affirm nor deny the possibility of knowledge but would remain peaceful, still waiting to see what might develop. The Pyrrhonist did not become inactive in this state of suspense but lived undogmatically according to appearances, customs, and natural inclinations.

PYTHAGOREANISM AND NEO-PYTHAGOREANISM

In the first half of the 4th century BCE, Tarentum, in southern Italy, rose into considerable significance. Under the political and spiritual leadership of the mathematician Archytas, a friend of Plato, the city became a new centre of Pythagoreanism, from which so-called acousmatics—Pythagoreans who did not sympathize with Archytas—went out travelling as mendicant ascetics all around the Greek-speaking world. The acousmatics seem to have preserved some early Pythagorean *Hieroi Logoi* ("Sacred Discourses") and ritual practices. Archytas himself, on the other hand, concentrated on scientific problems, and the organization of his Pythagorean brotherhood was evidently less rigorous than that of the early school. After the 380s there was a give-and-take between the school of Archytas and the Academy of Plato, a relationship that makes it almost impossible to disentangle the original achievements of Archytas from joint involvements.

Whereas the school of Archytas apparently sank into inactivity after the death of its founder (probably after 350 BCE), the Academics of the next generation continued "Pythagorizing" Platonic doctrines, such as that of the supreme One, the indefinite dyad (a metaphysical principle), and the tripartite soul. At the same time, various Peripatetics of the school of Aristotle, including Aristoxenus, collected Pythagorean legends and applied contemporary ethical notions to them. In the Hellenistic Age, the Academic and Peripatetic views gave rise to a rather fanciful antiquarian literature on Pythagoreanism. There also appeared a large and yet more heterogeneous mass of apocryphal writings falsely attributed to different Pythagoreans, as if attempts were being made to revive the school. The texts fathered on Archytas display Academic and Peripatetic philosophies mixed with some notions that were originally Pythagorean. Other texts were fathered on Pythagoras himself or on his immediate pupils, imagined or real. Some show, for instance, that Pythagoreanism had become confused with Orphism; others suggest that Pythagoras was considered a magician and an astrologist; there are also indications of Pythagoras "the athlete" and "the Dorian nationalist." But the anonymous authors of this pseudo-Pythagorean literature did not succeed in reestablishing the school, and the "Pythagorean" congregations formed in early imperial Rome seem to have had little in common with the original school of Pythagoreanism established in the late 6th century BCE; they were ritualistic sects that adopted, eclectically, various occult practices.

The acousmatics represent one of many schools of Neo-Pythagorean thought influenced by the works and philosophy of Pythagoras, shown above. SSPL/ Getty Images

With the ascetic sage Apollonius of Tyana, about the middle of the 1st century CE, a distinct Neo-Pythagorean trend appeared. Apollonius studied the Pythagorean legends of the previous centuries, created and propagated the ideal of a Pythagorean life—of occult wisdom, purity, universal tolerance, and approximation to the divine—and felt himself to be a reincarnation of Pythagoras. Through the activities of Neo-Pythagorean Platonists, such as Moderatus of Gades, a pagan trinitarian, and the arithmetician Nicomachus of Gerasa, both of the 1st century CE, and, in the 2nd or 3rd century, Numenius of Apamea, forerunner of Plotinus (an epoch-making elaborator of Platonism), Neo-Pythagoreanism gradually became a part of the expression of Platonism known as Neoplatonism; and it did so without having achieved a scholastic system of its own. The founder of a Syrian school of Neoplatonism, Iamblichus of Chalcis (c. 250–c. 330), a pupil of Porphyry (who in turn had been a pupil of Plotinus), thought of himself as a Pythagorean sage and about 300 CE wrote the last great synthesis of Pythagoreanism, in which most of the disparate post-classical traditions are reflected. It is characteristic of the Neo-Pythagoreans that they were chiefly interested in the Pythagorean way of life and in the pseudoscience of number mysticism. On a more popular level, Pythagoras and Archytas were remembered as magicians. Moreover, it has been suggested that Pythagorean legends were also influential in guiding the Christian monastic tradition.

NEOPLATONISM

Neoplatonism is the modern name given to the form of Platonism developed by Plotinus in the 3rd century CE and modified by his successors. It came to dominate the

Greek philosophical schools and remained predominant until the teaching of philosophy by pagans ended in the second half of the 6th century CE. It represents the final form of pagan Greek philosophy. It was not a mere syncretism (or combination of diverse beliefs) but a genuine, if one-sided, development of ideas to be found in Plato and earlier Platonism—though it incorporated important Aristotelian and Stoic elements as well. There is no real evidence for Oriental influence. A certain Gnostic (relating to intuitive knowledge acquired by privileged individuals and immune to empirical verification) tone or colouring sometimes may be discerned in the thought of Plotinus. But he was consciously a passionate opponent of Gnosticism, and in any case there was often a large element of popular Platonism in the Gnostic systems then current. Moreover, the theosophical works of the late 2nd century CE known as the *Chaldean Oracles*, which were taken as inspired authorities by the later Neoplatonists, seem to have been a hodgepodge of popular Greek religious philosophy.

Neoplatonism began as a complex (and in some ways ambiguous) philosophy and grew vigorously in a variety of forms over a long period; it is therefore not easy to generalize about it. But the leading ideas in the thought of philosophers who can properly be described as Neoplatonists seem always to have included the following:

1. There is a plurality of levels of being, arranged in hierarchical descending order, the last and lowest comprising the physical universe, which exists in time and space and is perceptible to the senses.
2. Each level of being is derived from its superior, a derivation that is not a process in time or space.
3. Each derived being is established in its own reality by turning back toward its superior in a movement

of contemplative desire, which is implicit in the original creative impulse of outgoing that it receives from its superior; thus the Neoplatonic universe is characterized by a double movement of outgoing and return.

4. Each level of being is an image or expression on a lower level of the one above it. The relation of archetype and image runs through all Neoplatonic schemes.

5. Degrees of being are also degrees of unity; as one goes down the scale of being there is greater multiplicity, more separateness, and increasing limitation—until the atomic individualization of the spatiotemporal world is reached.

6. The highest level of being, and through it all of what in any sense exists, derives from the ultimate principle, which is absolutely free from determinations and limitations and utterly transcends any conceivable reality, so that it may be said to be "beyond being." Because it has no limitations, it has no division, attributes, or qualifications; it cannot really be named, or even properly described as being, but may be called "the One" to designate its complete simplicity. It may also be called "the Good" as the source of all perfections and the ultimate goal of return, for the impulse of outgoing and return that constitutes the hierarchy of derived reality comes from and leads back to the Good.

7. Since this supreme principle is absolutely simple and undetermined (or devoid of specific traits), human knowledge of it must be radically different from any other kind of knowledge. It is not an object (a separate, determined, limited thing) and no predicates can be applied to it; hence it can be known only if it raises the mind to an

immediate union with itself, which cannot be imagined or described.

PLOTINUS AND HIS PHILOSOPHY

As far as is known, the originator of this distinctive kind of Platonism was Plotinus (205–270 CE). He had been the pupil at Alexandria of a self-taught philosopher called Ammonius, who also taught the Christian Origen and the latter's pagan namesake, and whose influence on his pupils seems to have been deep and lasting. But Ammonius wrote nothing; there are few reports of his views, and these are unreliable so that nothing is actually known about his thought. Plotinus must thus be regarded as the first Neoplatonist, and his collected works, the *Enneads* (Greek *enneas*, "set of nine"—six sets of nine treatises each, arranged by his disciple Porphyry), are the first and greatest collection of Neoplatonic writings.

Plotinus, like most ancient philosophers from Socrates on, was a religious and moral teacher as well as a professional philosopher engaged in the critical interpretation of a long and complicated school tradition. He was an acute critic and arguer, with an exceptional degree of intellectual honesty for his, or any, period; philosophy for him was not only a matter of abstract speculation but also a way of life in which, through an exacting intellectual and moral self-discipline and purification, those who are capable of the ascent can return to the source from which they came. His written works explain how from the eternal creative act—at once spontaneous and necessary—of that transcendent source, the One, or Good, proceeds the world of living reality, constituted by repeated double movements of outgoing and return in contemplation; and this account, showing the way for the human self—which can experience and be active on every level of being—to return to the One, is at the same time an exhortation to follow that way.

Plotinus always insisted that the One, or Good, is beyond the reach of thought or language; what he said about this supreme principle was intended only to point the mind along the way to it, not to describe or define it. But though no adequate concept or definition of the Good is possible, it was, nonetheless, for Plotinus a positive reality of superabundant excellence. Plotinus often spoke of it in extremely negative language, but his object in doing so was to stress the inadequacy of all of man's ways of thinking and speaking to express this supreme reality or to clarify the implications of the claim that the Good is absolutely one and undetermined, the source of all defined and limited realities.

The original creative or expressive act of the One is the first great derived reality, nous (which can be only rather inadequately translated as "Intellect" or "Spirit"); from this again comes Soul, which forms, orders, and maintains in being the material universe. It must be remembered that, to Plotinus, the whole process of generation is timeless; Nous and Soul are eternal, while time is the life of Soul as active in the physical world, and there never was a time when the material universe did not exist. The "levels of being," then, though distinct, are not separate but are all intimately present everywhere and in everyone. To ascend from Soul through Intellect to the One is not to travel in space but to awake to a new kind of awareness.

Intellect for Plotinus is at one and the same time thinker, thought, and object of thought; it is a mind that is perfectly one with its object. As object, it is the world of forms, the totality of real being in the Platonic sense. These forms, being one with Intellect and therefore with each other, are not merely objects but are living, thinking subjects, each not only itself but, in its contemplation, the whole. They are the archetypes and causes of the necessarily imperfect realities on lower levels, souls and the patterns or structures that make bodies what they are. Humans at their highest are intellects, or souls perfectly conformed to Intellect; they become aware of their intellectual nature when, passing not only beyond sense perception but beyond the discursive reasoning characteristic of the life of Soul, they immediately grasp eternal realities.

Soul for Plotinus is very much what it was for Plato, the intermediary between the worlds of Intellect and Sense and the representative of the former in the latter. It is produced by Intellect, as Intellect is by the One, by a double movement of outgoing and return in contemplation, but the relationship between the two is more intimate and the frontier less clearly defined. For Plotinus, as for Plato, the characteristic of the life of the Soul is movement, which is the cause of all other movements. The life of the Soul in this movement is time, and on it all physical movement depends. Soul both forms and rules the material universe from above; and in its lower, immanent phase, which Plotinus often calls nature, it acts as an indwelling principle of life and growth and produces the lowest forms, those of bodies. Below these lies the darkness of matter, the final absence of being, the absolute limit at which the expansion of the universe—from the One through diminishing degrees of reality and increasing degrees of multiplicity—comes to an end. Because of its utter negativity, such matter is for Plotinus the principle of evil; and although he does not really believe it to be an independent principle forming, with the Good, a dualism, his language about it often has a strongly dualistic flavour.

He was not, however, really dualistic in his attitude toward the material universe. He strongly maintained its goodness and beauty as the best possible work of Soul. It is a living organic whole, and its wholeness is the best possible (though very imperfect) reflection on the space-time level of the living unity in diversity of the world of forms in Intellect. It is held together in every part by a universal sympathy and harmony. In this harmony external evil and suffering take their place as necessary elements in the great pattern, the great dance of the universe. Evil and suffering can affect humans' lower selves but can only exceptionally, in the thoroughly depraved, touch their true, higher selves and so cannot interfere with the real well-being of the philosopher.

As souls within bodies, humans can exist on any level of the soul's experience and activity. (The descent of souls into bodies is for Plotinus—who had some difficulty in reconciling Plato's various statements on this point—both a fall and a necessary compliance with universal law.) The human individual can ascend through his own intellect to the level of universal Soul, become that whole that he already is potentially, and, in Soul, attain to Intellect itself; or he can isolate himself on the lower level, shutting himself up in the experiences, desires, and concerns of his lower nature. Philosophical conversion—the beginning of the ascent to the One—consists precisely in turning away, by a tremendous intellectual and moral effort, from the life of the body, dominating and rising above its desires, and "waking to another way of seeing, which everyone has but few use." This, Plotinus insisted, is possible while one is still in an earthly body and without neglecting the duties of one's embodied state. But the body and bodily life weight a person down and hamper him in his ascent. Plotinus' language when speaking of the body and the senses in this context is strongly dualistic and other-worldly. Platonists in general think much more dualistically about their own bodies than about the material universe as a whole. The physical world is seen positively as a noble image of the intelligible; the individual, earthly, animal body, on the contrary, tends to be regarded negatively as a hindrance to the intellectual and spiritual life.

When a person's philosophical conversion is complete and he has become Intellect, he can rise to that mystical union in which the One manifests his continual presence, carried on the surging current of the impulse of return to the source (in its strongest and final flow), the pure love of Intellect for the Good from which it immediately springs. There is no consciousness of duality in that union; the individual is not aware of himself; but neither is he destroyed or dissolved into the One—because even in the union he is still Intellect, though Intellect "out of itself," transcending its normal nature and activity. This mystical union for Plotinus was the focus of much of his effort and, for those of similar inclination, the source of the continuing power of his teaching. Philosophy for him was religion, the effort to actualize in oneself the great impulse of return to the Good, which constitutes reality on all its levels; and religion for him was philosophy. There was no room in his thought and practice for special revelation, grace, and repentance in the Christian sense, and little for external rites or ceremonies. For him the combination of moral purification and intellectual enlightenment, which only Platonic philosophy as he understood it could give, was the only way to union with the Good.

THE LATER NEOPLATONISTS

Porphyry (c. 234–c. 305 CE), a devout disciple of Plotinus and a careful editor of his works, occupied a special position in the development of later Neoplatonism. In some ways his thought paralleled that of the later pagan Neoplatonists, but in others it quite opposed them. The most distinctive features of his thought seem to have been an extreme spiritualism, an insistence, even sharper than that of Plotinus, on the "flight from the body" and—more philosophically important—a greater sympathy with the less sharply defined vertical hierarchies of the Platonists who had preceded Plotinus. Porphyry did not always clearly distinguish the One from Intellect. On the other hand, one may see in him the beginnings of the late Neoplatonic tendency to structure reality in both vertical and "horizontal" triads. Thus Being, Life, and Intellect are phases in the eternal self-determination of the ultimate reality. This triad became one of the most important elements in the complex metaphysical structures of the later Neoplatonists. But perhaps Porphyry's most important and influential contribution was the incorporation into Neoplatonism of Aristotle's logic, in particular the doctrine of the categories, with the characteristic Neoplatonic interpretation of them as terms signifying entities. Also of interest is his declaration of ideological war against the Christians, whose doctrines he attacked on both philosophical and exegetical grounds in a work of 15 books entitled *Against the Christians*.

Iamblichus (*c.* 250–*c.* 330 CE) seems to have been the originator of the type of Neoplatonism that came to dominate the Platonic schools in the 5th and 6th centuries CE. This kind of Neoplatonism sharpened and multiplied the distinctions between the levels of being. The basic position underlying its elaborations is one of extreme philosophical realism: it is assumed that the structure of reality corresponds so exactly to the way in which the mind works that there is a separate real entity corresponding to every distinction that it can make. In the fully developed late Neoplatonic system the first principle of reality, the ultimate One, was removed to an altogether ineffable transcendence, mitigated by two factors: the presence of the expressions or manifestations of its unifying power, the "henads"—identified with the gods of paganism—at every level of reality; and the possibility of return to absolute unification through the henad with which one is linked. Below the One a vast structure of triads, or trinities, reached down to the physical world; this was constructed by combining Plotinus' vertical succession of the levels of Being, Intellect, and Soul (much complicated by internal subdivision and the interposition at every stage of mediating hypostases, or underlying orders of nonmaterial reality) with another horizontal triadic structure, giving a timeless dynamic rhythm of outgoing and return, such as that already encountered in Porphyry.

Nearly all of Iamblichus' works have been lost, and his thought must be recovered from other sources. At present the main authority for this type of Platonism, and also for some of the later Neoplatonists, is Proclus (410–485 CE). Proclus appears to have codified later Platonism, but it is often impossible to tell which parts of his thought are original and which derive from his teachers Plutarch and Syrianus on the one hand and Porphyry and Iamblichus, from whom he quotes copiously but not always identifiably, and other earlier Platonists on the other hand. A carefully argued summary of the basic metaphysics of this kind of Neoplatonism may be found in Proclus' *Elements of Theology*, which exhibits the causal relationships of the several hierarchies that constituted his intelligible universe.

This later Neoplatonism aspired to be not only a complete and coherent metaphysical system but also a complete pagan theology, which is perhaps best seen in

Proclus' *Platonic Theology*. The maintenance and defense of the old religion in a world more and more intolerantly dominated by its triumphant rival, Christianity, was one of the main concerns of the Platonists after Plotinus. By the study and sometimes forced exegesis of Aristotle and then Plato, culminating in the *Timaeus* and *Parmenides*, of which they offered a variety of highly metaphysical interpretations totally unacceptable to Plato scholars, they believed it possible to arrive at a complete understanding of divine truth. This truth they held to be cryptically revealed by the gods themselves through the so-called theologians—the inspired authors of the Orphic poems and of the *Chaldean Oracles*, published in the second half of the 2nd century CE. Porphyry first gave some guarded and qualified recognition to them, but they were inspired scripture to Iamblichus, who wrote a work of at least 28 books on the subject, and his successors. Their view of the human soul was humbler than that of Plotinus. It was for them a spiritual being of lower rank, which had descended altogether into the material world, while for Plotinus a part remained above; they could not therefore aspire, like Plotinus, through philosophy alone, to that return to and unification with the divine that remained for them the goal of human life. Help from the gods was needed, and they believed that the gods in their love for men had provided it, giving to all things the power of return in prayer and implanting even in inanimate material things—herbs and stones and the like—sympathies and communications with the divine, which made possible the secret rites of theurgy, through which the divine gave the needed spiritual help by material means. Theurgy, though its procedures were generally those of late Greek magic, was thus not thought of merely as magic; in fact a higher and more intellectual theurgy was also practiced. The degree of attention paid to external rites varied considerably from philosopher to philosopher; there seem to have been thinkers even in the last generation of pagan Neoplatonists who had little use for or interest in such things and followed a mystical way much like that of Plotinus.

The different schools of late Neoplatonism seem to have differed less from each other than has sometimes been supposed. The school of Pergamum, founded by Aedesius, a pupil of Iamblichus, made perhaps the least contribution to the philosophical development of Neoplatonism, but it was not entirely given over to theurgy. Its greatest convert was the emperor Julian the Apostate, though he was not himself a distinguished philosopher. By the end of the 4th century CE the Platonic Academy at Athens had been reestablished and had become an institute for Neoplatonic teaching and research following the tradition of Iamblichus. It was particularly fervent and open in its paganism and attracted Christian hostility. Although maintaining itself for a surprisingly long time against this hostility, it eventually yielded to it and was probably closed by the Eastern Roman emperor Justinian in 529 CE. In the interim, however, it had produced the greatest and most influential systematic expositor of later Neoplatonism, Proclus. The head of the school at the time of its closing, Damascius, was also a notable philosopher. Another centre of Neoplatonism flourished at Gaza during the 5th and early 6th centuries; it was already Christian in its inspiration, though some of its members studied with the pagan Ammonius. The school of Alexandria in the 5th and 6th centuries does not seem to have differed very much from that of Athens, either in its fundamental philosophical outlook or in the main outline of its doctrines. In fact there was much interchange between the two. The Athenian Syrianus taught the Alexandrian Hermias, whose son Ammonius was taught by Proclus. Ammonius was the most influential of the Alexandrian

Platonists. His expositions of Aristotle were published mainly in the commentaries of the Christian heretic John Philoponus (late 5th to mid-6th century). Simplicius, the other great Aristotelian commentator, worked at Athens but, like Damascius, had studied with Ammonius. The Alexandrian concentration on Aristotle, which produced a vast body of learned but Neoplatonically coloured commentary on his treatises, has often been attributed to Christian pressure and attempts to compromise with the church; it may equally well have been due to the quality and extent of Proclus' published work on Plato. Although Philoponus' later philosophical work contains important Christian modifications, an openly pagan (and very inferior) philosopher, Olympiodorus, was still teaching at Alexandria well into the second half of the 6th century. Finally, in the 7th century, under Heraclius, after philosophical teaching had passed peacefully into Christian hands, the last known Alexandrian philosopher, the Christian Stephanus, was called to teach in the University of Constantinople.

CHAPTER 6

JEWISH AND CHRISTIAN PHILOSOPHY IN THE ANCIENT WORLD

W ell before the beginning of the Common Era, Jews with some Greek education had begun to make casual use of popular Greek philosophy in expounding their revealed religion: there are traces of this in the wisdom literature of the Hebrew Bible (Old Testament). In Paul's speech to the Areopagus in Acts 17, commonplaces of Stoic philosophy were employed for apologetic purposes. But, as far as is known, the first Jew who was really well-read in Greek philosophy and used it extensively in the exposition and defense of his traditional religion was Philo Judaeus (Philo of Alexandria [c. 15 BCE–after 45 CE]), an older contemporary of St. Paul. Philo expressed his philosophical religion in the form of lengthy allegorical commentaries on the Jewish Scriptures, especially on Genesis. In these he showed to his own satisfaction that the ancient revelation given to Moses accorded with the teaching of the best Greek philosophers, which, in his view, was later and derivative. The Greek philosophy that he preferred and found to be most in accordance with revelation was Platonism. Philo was neither approved of nor read by later orthodox Jews, but his influence on Greek-speaking and Greek-educated Christians from the 2nd century CE was great; and in

Paul, a convert to Christianity, was an active missionary during the 1st century CE. He was a significant Christian thinker whose writings and teachings resonate in the works of other philosophers like those of St. Augustine. Hulton Archive/Getty Images

important ways he determined the tone of their religious speculation.

Like Philo, the Christian Platonists gave primacy to revelation and regarded Platonic philosophy as the best available instrument for understanding and defending the teachings of Scripture and church tradition.

Although Stoicism had exerted a considerable influence on Christian ethical thinking (which has persisted to modern times), Stoic corporealism—the belief that God and the soul are bodies of a subtle and peculiar kind—repelled most Christians, and Stoic pantheism was incompatible with Christianity. The Platonism that the first Christian thinkers knew was of course Middle Platonism, not yet Neoplatonism. Its relatively straightforward theism and high moral tone suited their purposes excellently; and the influence of this older form of Platonism persisted through the 4th century and beyond, even after the works of Plotinus and Porphyry began to be read by Christians.

The first Christian to use Greek philosophy in the service of the Christian faith was Justin Martyr (martyred c. 165), whose passionate rejection of Greek polytheism, combined with an open and positive acceptance of the essentials of Platonic religious philosophy and an unshakable confidence in its harmony with Christian teaching, was to remain characteristic of the Christian Platonist tradition. This was carried on in the Greek-speaking world by Clement of Alexandria (c. 150–c. 215), a persuasive Christian humanist, and by the greatest of the Alexandrian Christian teachers, Origen (c. 185–254). Although Origen was consciously more hostile to and critical of Platonic philosophy than either Justin or Clement, he was, nonetheless, more deeply affected by it. He produced a synthesis of Christianity and late Middle Platonism of remarkable originality and power, which is the first great

Christian philosophical theology. In spite of subsequent condemnations of some of his alleged views, his influence on Christian thought was strong and lasting. The Greek philosophical theology that developed during the Trinitarian controversies over the relationships among the persons of the Godhead, which were settled at the ecumenical councils of Nicaea (325) and Constantinople (381), owed a great deal to Origen on both sides, orthodox and heretical. Its most important representatives on the orthodox side were the three Christian Platonist theologians of Cappadocia, Basil of Caesarea (c. 329–379), Gregory of Nazianzus (c. 330–c. 389), and Basil's brother Gregory of Nyssa (c. 335–c. 394). Of these three, Gregory of Nyssa was the most powerful and original thinker (as well as the closest to Origen). He was the first great theologian of mystical experience, at once Platonic and profoundly Christian, and he exerted a strong influence on later Greek Christian thought.

At some time between the period of the Cappadocian Fathers and the early years of the 6th century, a new turn was given to Christian Platonism by the remarkable writer who chose to publish his works under the name of St. Paul's convert at Athens, Dionysius the Areopagite. The kind of Platonism that the Pseudo-Dionysius employed for his theological purposes was the 5th-century Neoplatonism that is best represented by Proclus. Almost everything about this mysterious author is vigorously disputed by scholars. But there can be no doubt about the influence that his system of the hierarchic universe exerted upon later Christian thought; his vision of human ascent through it—carried up by divine love, to pass beyond all hierarchy and all knowledge into the darkness of the mystical union with God—had its impact both in the East, where one of the greatest of Greek Christian Platonist thinkers, Maximus the Confessor (c. 580–662), was deeply

Overhead view of the church of St. Gregory of Nazianzus in the Nevsehir province of Turkey (once known as Cappadocia), the region where all three Cappadocian Fathers once lived and defended orthodoxy against Arianism.
John Elk III/Lonely Planet Images/Getty Images

influenced by the Dionysian writings and commented extensively upon them, and in the West, where they became known and were translated into Latin in the 9th century. In the Latin West there was more than one kind of Christian Platonism. An impressive and extremely difficult philosophical theology, employing ideas approximating Porphyry's version of Neoplatonism to explain and defend the orthodox doctrine of the Trinity, was produced in the second half of the 4th century by the rhetorician and grammarian Marius Victorinus. A strong and simple Platonic theism and morality, which had a great influence in the Middle Ages, was nobly expressed in the final work of the last great philosopher-statesman of the ancient world, Boethius (*c.* 470–524). This was the *Consolation of Philosophy*, written in prison while its author was under sentence of death. Boethius was also influential in the medieval West through his translations of Aristotle's logical works, especially the *Categories* together with Porphyry's *Isagoge* ("Introduction"), on which he in turn produced two commentaries.

But the Christian Platonism that had the widest, deepest, and most lasting influence in the West was that of St. Augustine of Hippo (354–430). Each of the great Christian Platonists understood Platonism and applied it to the understanding of his faith in his own individual way, and of no one of them was this truer than of Augustine with his extremely strong personality and distinctive religious history. Augustine's thought was not merely a subspecies of Christian Platonism but something unique—Augustinianism. Nonetheless, the reading of Plotinus and Porphyry (in Latin translations) had a decisive influence on his religious and intellectual development, and he was more deeply and directly affected by Neoplatonism than any of his Western contemporaries and successors.

PHILO JUDAEUS

Philo Judaeus, a Greek-speaking Jewish philosopher and the most important representative of Hellenistic Judaism, was born in Alexandria, Egypt, between 15 and 10 BCE and died there between 45 and 50 CE. His writings provide the clearest view of this development of Judaism in the Diaspora. As the first to attempt to synthesize revealed faith and philosophical reason, he occupies a unique position in the history of philosophy. He is also regarded by Christians as a forerunner of Christian theology.

LIFE AND BACKGROUND

Little is known of the life of Philo. Josephus, the historian of the Jews who also lived in the 1st century, says that Philo's family surpassed all others in the nobility of its lineage. His father had apparently played a prominent role in Palestine before moving to Alexandria. Philo's brother Alexander Lysimachus, who was a general tax administrator in charge of customs in Alexandria, was the richest man in the city and indeed must have been one of the richest men in the Hellenistic world, because Josephus says that he gave a huge loan to the wife of the Jewish king Agrippa I and that he contributed the gold and silver with which nine huge gates of the Temple in Jerusalem were overlaid. Alexander was also extremely influential in Roman imperial circles, being an old friend of the emperor Claudius and having acted as guardian for the Emperor's mother.

The Jewish community of Alexandria, to judge from the language of the Jewish papyri and inscriptions, had for nearly three centuries been almost exclusively Greek-speaking and indeed regarded the Septuagint (the 3rd-century-BCE translation of the Hebrew Bible into

PHILON JVIF.
Chap. 39.

OMBIEN que (fuyuant l'ancien prouer-
be) à bon vin ne faille leuer vn bouchon, ny
pareillement vn homme de foy vertueux &
loüable ayt befoing eftre loüé par autruy, la
vertu fe contantant de foy-mefmes, neant-
moins pour ne laiffer ce pourtrait fans eftre
accompaigné de quelque declaration, con-
tenant la vie, les actes infignes, & ferueur in-
croyable, que Philon furnommé le Iuif a delaiffé à la pofterité, ie fup- *Lieu de la*
poferay en premier lieu, qu'il fut natif d'Alexandrie, ville renommée *naiffance de Philon.*

Philo Judaeus, whose works were unique in their attempt to reconcile Judaism and Greek philosophy and were significant also for their influence on Christian theology. Library of Congress Prints & Photographs Division

Greek) as divinely inspired. During the century and a half before Philo's birth, Alexandria had been the home of a number of Jewish writers whose works exist now only in fragments. These men were often influenced by the Greek culture in which they lived and wrote apologies for Judaism.

The Alexandrian Jews were eager to enroll their children of secondary school age in Greek gymnasiums; in them, Jews were certainly called upon to make compromises with their traditions. It may be assumed that Philo was a product of such an education: he mentions a wide range of Greek writers, especially the epic and dramatic poets; he was intimately acquainted with the techniques of the Greek rhetorical schools; and he praises the gymnasium. Philo's education, like that which he ascribes to Moses, most probably consisted of arithmetic, geometry, astronomy, harmonics, philosophy, grammar, rhetoric, and logic.

Like the cultured Greeks of his day, Philo often attended the theatre, though it had distinctly religious connotations, and he noted the different effects of the same music on various members of the audience and the enthusiasm of the audience for a tragedy of Euripides. He was a keen observer of boxing contests and attended chariot races as well. He also mentions the frequency with which he attended costly suppers with their lavish entertainment.

Philo says nothing of his own Jewish education. The only mention of Jewish education in his work indicates how relatively weak it must have been, because he speaks only of Jewish schools that met on the Sabbath for lectures on ethics. That he was far from the Palestinian Hellenizers and that he regarded himself as an observant Jew is clear, however, from his statement that one should not omit the observance of any of the Jewish customs that have been divinely ordained. Philo is critical both of those who took the Bible too literally and thus encountered theological difficulties, particularly anthropomorphisms—describing God in terms of human characteristics—and those who went to excesses in their allegorical interpretation of the laws, with the resulting conclusion, anticipating St. Paul, that because the ceremonial laws were only a parable, they need no longer be obeyed. Philo says nothing of his own religious practices, except that he made a festival pilgrimage to Jerusalem, though he nowhere indicates whether he made more than one such visit.

In the eyes of the Palestinian rabbis, the Alexandrian Jews were particularly known for their cleverness in posing puzzles and for their sharp replies. As the largest repository of Jewish law apart from the Talmud before the Middle Ages, Philo's work is of special importance to those who wish to discern the relationship of Palestine and the Diaspora in the realm of law (*halakah*) and ritual observance. Philo's exposition of the law may represent either an academic discussion giving an ideal description of Jewish law or the actual practice in the Jewish courts in Egypt. On the whole, Philo is in accord with the prevailing Palestinian point of view; nonetheless he differs from it in numerous details and is often dependent upon Greek and Roman law.

That Philo experienced some sort of identity crisis is indicated by a passage in his *On the Special Laws*. In this work, he describes his longing to escape from worldly cares to the contemplative life, his joy at having succeeded in doing so (perhaps with the Egyptian Jewish ascetic sect of the Therapeutae described in his treatise *On the Contemplative Life*), and his renewed pain at being forced once again to participate in civic turmoil. Philo appears to have been dissatisfied with his life in the bustling metropolis of Alexandria: he praises the Essenes—a Jewish sect who lived in monastic communities in the Dead Sea area—for avoiding large cities because of the iniquities that had become inveterate among city dwellers, for living an agricultural life, and for disdaining wealth.

The one identifiable event in Philo's life occurred in the year 39 or 40, when, after a pogrom against the Jews in Alexandria, he headed an embassy to the emperor Caligula asking him to reassert Jewish rights granted by the Ptolemies (rulers of Egypt) and confirmed by the emperor Augustus. Philo was prepared to answer the charge of disloyalty levelled against the Jews by the notorious anti-Semite Apion, a Greek grammarian, when the emperor cut him short. Thereupon Philo told his fellow delegates not to be discouraged because God would punish Caligula, who, shortly thereafter, was indeed assassinated.

WORKS

Philo's genuine works may be classified into three groups:

1. Scriptural essays and homilies based on specific verses or topics of the Pentateuch (the first five books of the Bible), especially Genesis. The most important of the 25 extant treatises in this group are *Allegories of the Laws,* a commentary on Genesis, and *On the Special Laws,* an exposition of the laws in the Pentateuch.
2. General philosophical and religious essays. These include *That Every Good Man Is Free,* proving the Stoic paradox that only the wise person is free; *On the Eternity of the World,* perhaps not genuine, proving, particularly in opposition to the Stoics, that the world is uncreated and indestructible; *On Providence,* extant in Armenian, a dialogue between Philo, who argues that God is providential in his

concern for the world, and Alexander, presumably
Philo's nephew Tiberius Julius Alexander, who
raises doubts; and *On Alexander,* extant in Armenian,
concerning the irrational souls of animals.

3. Essays on contemporary subjects. These include *On
the Contemplative Life,* a eulogy of the Therapeutae
sect; the fragmentary *Hypothetica* ("Suppositions"),
actually a defense of the Jews against anti-Semitic
charges to which Josephus' treatise *Against Apion*
bears many similarities; *Against Flaccus,* on the
crimes of Aulus Avillius Flaccus, the Roman governor of Egypt, against the Alexandrian Jews and on
his punishment; and *On the Embassy to Gaius,* an
attack on the emperor Caligula (i.e., Gaius) for his
hostility toward the Alexandrian Jews and an
account of the unsuccessful embassy to the emperor
headed by Philo.

A number of works ascribed to Philo are almost certainly spurious. Most important of these is *Biblical
Antiquities,* an imaginative reconstruction of Jewish history
from Adam to the death of Saul, the first king of Israel.

Philo's works are rambling, having little sense of form;
repetitious; artificially rhetorical; and almost devoid of a
sense of humour. His style is generally involved, allusive,
strongly tinged with mysticism, and often obscure; this
may be a result of a deliberate attempt on his part to dis-
courage all but the initiated few.

THE ORIGINALITY OF HIS THOUGHT

The key influences on Philo's philosophy were Plato,
Aristotle, the Neo-Pythagoreans, the Cynics, and the
Stoics. Philo's basic philosophic outlook is Platonic, so
much so that Jerome and other Church Fathers quote the

apparently widespread saying: "Either Plato philonizes or Philo platonizes." Philo's reverence for Plato, particularly for the *Symposium* and the *Timaeus,* is such that he never took open issue with him, as he did with the Stoics and other philosophers. But Philo is hardly a plagiarist; he made modifications in Plato's theories. To Aristotle he was indebted primarily in matters of cosmology and ethics. To the Neo-Pythagoreans, who had grown in importance during the century before Philo, he was particularly indebted for his views on the mystic significance of numbers, especially the number seven, and the scheme of a peculiar, self-disciplined way of life as a preparation for immortality. The Cynics, with their diatribes, influenced him in the form of his sermons. Although Philo more often employed the terminology of the Stoics than that of any other school, he was critical of their thoughts.

In the past, scholars attempted to diminish Philo's importance as a theological thinker and to present him merely as a preacher, but in the mid-20th century H.A. Wolfson, an American scholar, demonstrated Philo's originality as a thinker. In particular, Philo was the first to show the difference between the knowability of God's existence and the unknowability of his essence. Again, in his view of God, Philo was original in insisting on an individual Providence able to suspend the laws of nature in contrast to the prevailing Greek philosophical view of a universal Providence who is himself subject to the unchanging laws of nature. As a Creator, God made use of assistants: hence the plural "Let us make man" in Genesis, chapter 1. Philo did not reject the Platonic view of a preexistent matter but insisted that this matter too was created. Similarly, Philo reconciled his Jewish theology with Plato's theory of forms in an original way: he posited the forms as God's eternal thoughts, which God then created as real beings before he created the world.

Philo saw the cosmos as a great chain of being presided over by the Logos, a term going back to pre-Socratic philosophy, which is the mediator between God and the world, though at one point he identifies the Logos as a second God. Philo departed from Plato principally in using the term Logos for the form of forms and for the forms as a whole and in his statement that the Logos is the place of the intelligible world. In anticipation of Christian doctrine he called the Logos the first-begotten Son of God, the man of God, the image of God, and second to God.

Philo was also novel in his exposition of the mystic love of God that God has implanted in humans and through which humans become Godlike. According to some scholars, Philo used the terminology of the pagan religions and mystery cults, including the term *enthousiasmos* ("having God within one"), merely because it was part of the common speech of the day; but there is nothing inherently contradictory in Judaism in the combination of mysticism and legalism in the same thinker. The influence of the mystic notions of Platonism, especially of the *Symposium,* and of the popular mystery cults on Philo's attempt to present Judaism as the one true mystery is hardly superficial; indeed, Philo is a major source of knowledge of the doctrines of these mystery cults, notably that of rebirth. Perhaps, through his mystic presentation of Judaism, Philo hoped to enable Judaism in the Diaspora to compete with the mystery religions in its proselyting efforts, as well as in its attempts to hold on to its adherents. That he was essentially in the mainstream of Judaism, however, is indicated by his respect for the literal interpretation of the Bible, his denunciation of the extreme allegorists, and his failure to mention any specific rites of initiation for proselytes, as well as the lack of evidence that he was himself a devotee of a particular mystery cult.

The purpose of what Philo called mystic "sober intoxication" was to lead one out of the material into the eternal world. Like Plato, Philo regarded the body as the prison house of the soul, and in his dualism of body and soul, as in his description of the flight from the self, the contrast between God and the world, and the yearning for a direct experience of God, he anticipated much of Gnosticism, a dualistic religion that became important in the 2nd century BCE. But unlike all the Greek philosophers, with the exception of the Epicureans, who believed in limited freedom of will, Philo held that humans are completely free to act against all the laws of their own nature.

In his ethical theory Philo described two virtues, under the heading of justice, that are otherwise unknown in Greek philosophical literature—religious faith and humanity. Again, for him repentance was a virtue, whereas for other Greek philosophers it was a weakness. Perfect happiness comes, however, not through humans' own efforts to achieve virtue but only through the grace of God.

In his political theory Philo often said that the best form of government is democracy; but for him democracy was far from mob rule, which he denounced as the worst of polities, perhaps because he saw the Alexandrian mob in action. For Philo democracy meant not a particular form of government but due order under any form of government in which everyone is equal before the law. From this point of view, the Mosaic constitution, which embodies the best elements of all forms of government, is the ideal. Indeed, the ultimate goal of history is that the whole world be a single state under a democratic constitution.

SAINT AMBROSE

St. Ambrose (Latin: Ambrosius) was born in 339 CE in Augusta Treverorum in Gaul (present-day Trier, in southwestern Germany) and died in 397 in Milan. He was a bishop of Milan, a theologian and biblical critic who incorporated Neoplatonic doctrines into his exegesis of Scripture, and an initiator of ideas that provided a model for medieval conceptions of church-state relations. His literary works have been acclaimed as masterpieces of Latin eloquence, and his musical accomplishments are remembered in his hymns. Ambrose is also remembered as the teacher who

St. Ambrose, detail of a fresco by Pinturicchio, 1480s; in Santa Maria del Popolo, Rome. Alinari/Art Resource, New York

converted and baptized St. Augustine of Hippo, the great Christian theologian, and as a model bishop who viewed the church as rising above the ruins of the Roman Empire.

EARLY CAREER

Although Ambrose, the second son of the Roman prefect (viceroy) of Gaul, was born in the official residence at Augusta Treverorum, his father died soon afterward, and Ambrose was reared in Rome, in a palace frequented by the clergy, by his widowed mother and his elder sister Marcellina, a nun. Duly promoted to the governorship of Aemilia-Liguria in *c.* 370, he lived at Milan and was unexpectedly acclaimed as their bishop by the people of the city in 374.

Ambrose, a popular outsider, chosen as a compromise candidate to avoid a disputed election, changed from an unbaptized layman to a bishop in eight days. Coming from a well-connected but obscure senatorial family, Ambrose could be ignored as a provincial governor; as bishop of Milan he was able to dominate the cultural and political life of his age.

ECCLESIASTICAL ADMINISTRATIVE ACCOMPLISHMENTS

An imperial court frequently sat in Milan. In confrontations with this court, Ambrose showed a directness that combined the republican ideal of the prerogatives of a Roman senator with a sinister vein of demagoguery. In 384 he secured the rejection of an appeal for tolerance by pagan members of the Roman senate, whose spokesman, Quintus Aurelius Symmachus, was his relative. In 385–386 he refused to surrender a church for the use of Arian heretics. In 388 he rebuked the emperor Theodosius for having punished a bishop who had burnt a Jewish synagogue. In 390 he imposed public penance on Theodosius for having punished a riot in Thessalonica by a massacre of its citizens. These unprecedented interventions were palliated by Ambrose's loyalty and resourcefulness as a diplomat, notably in 383 and 386 by his official visits to the usurper Maximus at Trier. In his letters and in his funeral orations on the emperors Valentinian II and Theodosius—*De obitu Valentiniani consolatio* (392) and *De obitu Theodosii* (395)—Ambrose established the medieval concept of a Christian emperor as a dutiful son of the church "serving under orders from Christ," and so subject to the advice and strictures of his bishop.

LITERARY AND MUSICAL ACCOMPLISHMENTS

Ambrose's relations with the emperors formed only part of his commanding position among the lay governing class of Italy. He rapidly absorbed the most up-to-date Greek learning, Christian and pagan alike—notably the works of Philo, Origen, and St. Basil of Caesarea and of the pagan Neoplatonist Plotinus. This learning he used in sermons expounding the Bible and, especially, in defending the "spiritual" meaning of the Hebrew Bible by erudite philosophical allegory—notably in the *Hexaëmeron* ("On the Six Days of Creation") and in sermons on the patriarchs (of which *De Isaac et anima* ["On Isaac and the Soul"] and *De bono mortis* ["On the Goodness of Death"] betray a deep acquaintance with Neoplatonic mystical language). Sermons, the dating of which unfortunately remains uncertain, were Ambrose's main literary output. They were acclaimed as masterpieces of Latin eloquence, and they remain a quarry for students of the transmission of Greek philosophy and theology in the West. By such sermons Ambrose gained his most notable convert, Augustine, afterward bishop of Hippo in North Africa and destined, like Ambrose, to be revered as a doctor (teacher) of the church. Augustine went to Milan as a skeptical professor of rhetoric in 384; when he left, in 388, he had been baptized by Ambrose and was indebted to Ambrose's Catholic Neoplatonism, which provided a philosophical base that eventually transformed Christian theology.

Ambrose provided educated Latins with an impeccably classical version of Christianity. His work on the moral obligations of the clergy, *De officiis ministrorum* (386), is skillfully modelled on Cicero's *De officiis*. He sought to replace the heroes of Rome with Hebrew Bible saints as models of behaviour for a Christianized aristocracy. By letters, visitations, and nominations he strengthened this aristocratic Christianity in the northern Italian towns that he had once ruled as a Roman governor.

In Milan, Ambrose "bewitched" the populace by introducing new Eastern melodies and by composing beautiful hymns, notably "Aeterne rerum Conditor" ("Framer of the earth and sky") and "Deus Creator omnium" ("Maker of all things, God most high"). He spared no pains in instructing candidates for Baptism. He denounced social abuses (notably in the sermons *De Nabuthe* ["On Naboth"]) and frequently secured pardon for condemned men. He advocated the most austere asceticism: noble families were reluctant to let their marriageable daughters attend the sermons in which he urged upon them the crowning virtue of virginity.

EVALUATIONS AND INTERPRETATIONS

Ambrose's reputation after his death was unchallenged. For Augustine, he was the model bishop: a biography was written in 412 by Paulinus, deacon of Milan, at Augustine's instigation. To Augustine's opponent, Pelagius, Ambrose was "the flower of Latin eloquence." Of his sermons, the *Expositio evangelii secundum Lucam* (390; "Exposition of the Gospel According to Luke") was widely circulated.

Yet, Ambrose is a Janus-like figure. He imposed his will on emperors. But he never considered himself as a precursor of a polity in which the church dominated the state: for he acted from a traditional fear that Christianity might yet be eclipsed by a pagan nobility and Catholicism uprooted in Milan by Arian courtiers. His attitude to the learning he used was similarly old-fashioned. Pagans and heretics, he said, "dyed their impieties in the vats of philosophy"; yet his sermons betray the pagan mysticism of Plotinus in its most unmuted tints. In a near-contemporary mosaic in the chapel of St. Satiro in the church of St. Ambrogio, Milan, Ambrose appears as he wished to be seen: a simple Christian bishop clasping the book of Gospels. Yet the manner in which he set about his duties as a bishop ensured that, to use his own image, the Catholic Church would rise "like a growing moon" above the ruins of the Roman Empire.

SAINT AUGUSTINE

St. Augustine, also known as St. Augustine of Hippo, was born on Nov. 13, 354, in Tagaste, Numidia (now Souk Ahras, Algeria), and died on Aug. 28, 430, in Hippo Regius (now Annaba, Algeria). He was bishop of Hippo from 396 to 430, one of the Latin Fathers of the Church, one of the Doctors of the Church, and perhaps the most significant Christian thinker after St. Paul. Augustine's adaptation of classical thought to Christian teaching created a theological system of great power and lasting influence. His numerous written works, the most important of which are *Confessions* and *City of God*, shaped the practice of biblical exegesis and helped lay the foundation for much of medieval and modern Christian thought.

Augustine is remarkable for what he did and extraordinary for what he wrote. If none of his written works had survived, he would still have been a figure to be reckoned with, but his stature would have been more nearly that of some of his contemporaries. However, more than five million words of his writings survive, virtually all displaying the strength and sharpness of his mind (and some limitations of range and learning) and some possessing the rare power to attract and hold the attention of readers in both his day and ours. His distinctive theological style shaped Latin Christianity in a way surpassed only by scripture

St. Augustine working in his study. SuperStock/Getty Images

itself. His work continues to hold contemporary relevance, in part because of his membership in a religious group that was dominant in the West in his time and remains so today.

Intellectually, Augustine represents the most influential adaptation of the ancient Platonic tradition with Christian ideas that ever occurred in the Latin Christian world. Augustine received the Platonic past in a far more limited and diluted way than did many of his Greek-speaking contemporaries, but his writings were so widely read and imitated throughout Latin Christendom that his particular synthesis of Christian, Roman, and Platonic traditions defined the terms for much later tradition and debate. Both modern Roman Catholic and Protestant Christianity owe much to Augustine, though in some ways each community has at times been embarrassed to own up to that allegiance in the face of irreconcilable elements in his thought. For example, Augustine has been cited as both a champion of human freedom and an articulate defender of divine predestination, and his views on sexuality were humane in intent but have often been received as oppressive in effect.

LIFE

Augustine's birthplace, Tagaste, was a modest Roman community in a river valley 40 miles (64 km) from the African coast. It lay just a few miles short of the point where the veneer of Roman civilization thinned out in the highlands of Numidia in the way the American West opens before a traveler leaving the Mississippi River valley. Augustine's parents were of the respectable class of Roman society, free to live on the work of others, but their means were sometimes straitened. They managed, sometimes on borrowed money, to acquire a first-class education for Augustine, and, although he had at least one brother and one sister, he seems to have been the only child sent off to be educated. He studied first in Tagaste, then in the nearby university town of Madauros, and finally at Carthage, the great city of Roman Africa. After a brief stint teaching in Tagaste, he returned to Carthage to teach rhetoric, the premier science for the Roman gentleman, and he was evidently very good at it.

While still at Carthage, he wrote a short philosophical book aimed at displaying his own merits and advancing his career; unfortunately, it is lost. At the age of 28, restless and ambitious, Augustine left Africa in 383 to make his career in Rome. He taught there briefly before landing a plum appointment as imperial professor of rhetoric at Milan. The customary residence of the emperor at the time, Milan was the de facto capital of the Western Roman Empire and the place where careers were best made. Augustine tells us that he, and the many family members with him, expected no less than a provincial governorship as the eventual—and lucrative—reward for his merits.

Augustine's career, however, ran aground in Milan. After only two years there, he resigned his teaching post and, after some soul-searching and apparent idleness, made his way back to his native town of Tagaste. There he passed the time as a cultured squire, looking after his family property, raising the son, Adeodatus, left him by his long-term lover (her name is unknown) taken from the lower classes, and continuing his literary pastimes. The death of that son while still an adolescent left Augustine with no obligation to hand on the family property, and so he disposed of it and found himself, at age 36, literally pressed into service against his will as a junior clergyman in the coastal city of Hippo, north of Tagaste.

The transformation was not entirely surprising. Augustine had always been a dabbler in one form or another of the Christian religion, and the collapse of his career at Milan was associated with an intensification of religiosity. All his writings from that time onward were driven by his allegiance to a particular form of Christianity both orthodox and intellectual. His coreligionists in North Africa accepted his distinctive stance and style with some difficulty, and Augustine chose to associate himself with the "official" branch of Christianity, approved by emperors and reviled by the most enthusiastic and numerous branches of the African church. Augustine's literary and intellectual abilities, however, gave him the power to articulate his vision of Christianity in a way that set him apart from his African contemporaries. His unique gift was the ability to write at a high theoretical level for the most discerning readers and still be able to deliver sermons with fire and fierceness in an idiom that a less cultured audience could admire.

Made a "presbyter" (roughly, a priest, but with less authority than modern clergy of that title) at Hippo in 391, Augustine became bishop there in 395 or 396 and spent the rest of his life in that office. Hippo was a trading city, without the wealth and culture of Carthage or Rome, and Augustine was never entirely at home there. He would travel to Carthage for several months of the year to pursue ecclesiastical business in a milieu more welcoming to his talents than that of his adopted home city.

Augustine's educational background and cultural milieu trained him for the art of rhetoric: declaring the power of the self through speech that differentiated the speaker from his fellows and swayed the crowd to follow his views. That Augustine's training and natural talent coincided is best seen in an episode when he was in his early 60s and found himself quelling by force of personality and words an incipient riot while visiting the town of Caesarea Mauretanensis. The style of the rhetorician carried over in his ecclesiastical persona throughout his career. He was never without controversies to fight, usually with others of his own religion. In his years of rustication and early in his time at Hippo, he wrote book after book attacking Manichaeism, a Christian sect he had joined in his late teens and left 10 years later when it became impolitic to remain with them. For the next 20 years, from the 390s to the 410s, he was preoccupied with the struggle to make his own brand of Christianity prevail over all others in Africa. The native African Christian tradition had fallen afoul of the Christian emperors who succeeded Constantine (reigned 305–337) and was reviled as schismatic; it was branded with the name of Donatism after Donatus, one of its early leaders. Augustine and his chief colleague in the official church, Bishop Aurelius of Carthage, fought a canny and relentless campaign against it with their books, with their recruitment of support among church leaders, and with careful appeal to Roman officialdom. In 411 the reigning emperor sent an official representative to Carthage to settle the quarrel. A public debate held in three sessions during June 1–8 and attended by hundreds of bishops on each side ended with a ruling in favour of the official church. The ensuing legal restrictions on Donatism decided the struggle in favour of Augustine's party.

Even then, approaching his 60th year, Augustine found—or manufactured—a last great challenge for himself. Taking umbrage at the implications of the teachings of a traveling society preacher named Pelagius, Augustine gradually worked himself up to a polemical fever over ideas that Pelagius may or may not have espoused. Other churchmen of the time were perplexed and reacted with some caution to Augustine, but he persisted, even reviving the battle against austere monks and dignified bishops through the 420s. At the time of his death, he was at work on a vast and shapeless attack on the last and most urbane of his opponents, the Italian bishop Julian of Eclanum.

Through these years, Augustine had carefully built for himself a reputation as a writer throughout Africa and beyond. His careful cultivation of selected correspondents had made his name known in Gaul, Spain, Italy, and the Middle East, and his books were widely circulated throughout the Mediterranean world. In his last years he compiled a careful catalog of his books, annotating them with bristling defensiveness to deter charges of inconsistency. He had opponents, many of them heated in their attacks on him, but he usually retained their respect by the power and effectiveness of his writing.

CHIEF WORKS

Two of Augustine's works stand out above the others for their lasting influence, but they have had very different fates. *City of God* was widely read in Augustine's time and throughout the Middle Ages and still demands attention today, but it is impossible to read without a determined effort to place it in its historical context. The *Confessions* was not much read in the first centuries of the Middle Ages, but from the 12th century onward it has been continuously read as a vivid portrayal of an individual's struggle for self-definition in the presence of a powerful God.

CONFESSIONS

Although autobiographical narrative makes up much of the first 9 of the 13 books of Augustine's *Confessiones* (397; *Confessions*), autobiography is incidental to the main purpose of the work. For Augustine *confessions* is a catchall term for acts of religiously authorized speech: praise of God, blame of self, confession of faith. The book is a richly textured meditation by a middle-aged man (Augustine was in his early 40s when he wrote it) on the course and meaning of his own life. The dichotomy between past odyssey and present position of authority as bishop is emphasized in numerous ways in the book, not least in that what begins as a narrative of childhood ends with an extended and very churchy discussion of the book of Genesis—the progression is from the beginnings of a man's life to the beginnings of human society.

Between those two points the narrative of sin and redemption holds most readers' attention. Those who seek to find in it the memoirs of a great sinner are invariably disappointed, indeed often puzzled at the minutiae of failure that preoccupy the author. Of greater significance is the account of redemption. Augustine is especially influenced by the powerful intellectual preaching of the suave and diplomatic Bishop Ambrose, who reconciles for him the attractions of the intellectual and social culture of antiquity, in which Augustine was brought up and of which he was a master, and the spiritual teachings of Christianity. The link between the two was Ambrose's exposition, and Augustine's reception, of a selection of the doctrines of Plato, as mediated in late antiquity by the school of Neoplatonism. Augustine heard Ambrose and read, in Latin translation, some of the exceedingly difficult works of Plotinus and Porphyry; he acquired from them an intellectual vision of the fall and rise of the soul of man, a vision he found confirmed in the reading of the Bible proposed by Ambrose.

Religion for Augustine, however, was never merely a matter of the intellect. The seventh book of the *Confessions* recounts a perfectly satisfactory intellectual conversion, but the extraordinary eighth book takes him one necessary step further. Augustine could not bring himself to seek the ritual purity of baptism without cleansing himself of the desires of the flesh to an extreme degree. For him, baptism required renunciation of sexuality in all its express manifestations. The narrative of the *Confessions* shows Augustine forming the will to renounce sexuality through a reading of the letters of Paul. The decisive scene occurs in a garden in Milan, where a child's voice seems to bid Augustine to "take up and read," whereupon he finds in Paul's writings the inspiration to adopt a life of chastity.

The rest of the *Confessions* is mainly a meditation on how the continued study of scripture and pursuit of divine wisdom are still inadequate for attaining perfection and how, as bishop, Augustine makes peace with his imperfections. It is drenched in language from the Bible and is a work of great force and artistry.

CITY OF GOD

Fifteen years after Augustine wrote the *Confessions*, at a time when he was bringing to a close (and invoking government power to do so) his long struggle with the Donatists but before he had worked himself up to action against the Pelagians, the Roman world was shaken by news of a military action in Italy. A ragtag army under the leadership of Alaric, a general of Germanic ancestry and thus credited with leading a "barbarian" band, had been seeking privileges from the empire for many years, making from time to time extortionate raids against populous and prosperous areas. Finally, in 410, his forces attacked and seized the city of Rome itself, holding it for several days before decamping to the south of Italy. The military significance of the event was nil—such was the disorder of Roman government that other war bands would hold provinces hostage more and more frequently, and this particular band would wander for another decade before settling mainly in Spain and the south of France. But the symbolic effect of seeing the city of Rome taken by outsiders for the first time since the Gauls had done so in 390 BCE shook the secular confidence of many thoughtful people across the Mediterranean. Coming as it did less than 20 years after the decisive edict against "paganism" by the emperor Theodosius I in 391, it was followed by speculation that perhaps the Roman Empire had mistaken its way with the gods. Perhaps the new Christian god was not as powerful as he seemed. Perhaps the old gods had done a better job of protecting their followers.

It is hard to tell how seriously or widely such arguments were made; paganism by this time was in disarray, and Christianity's hold on the reins of government was unshakable. But Augustine saw in the murmured doubts a splendid polemical occasion he had long sought, and so he leapt to the defense of God's ways. That his readers and the doubters whose murmurs he had heard were themselves pagans is unlikely. At the very least, it is clear that his intended audience comprised many people who were at least outwardly affiliated with the Christian church. During the next 15 years, working meticulously through a lofty architecture of argument, he outlined a new way to understand human society, setting up the City of God over and against the City of Man. Rome was dethroned—and the sack of the city shown to be of no spiritual importance—in favour of the heavenly Jerusalem, the true home and source of citizenship for all Christians. The City of Man was doomed to disarray, and wise men would, as it were, keep their passports in order as citizens of the City above, living in this world as pilgrims longing to return home.

De civitate Dei contra paganos (413–426/427; *City of God*) is divided into 22 books. The first 10 refute the claims to divine power of various pagan communities. The last 12 retell the biblical story of mankind from Genesis to the Last Judgment, offering what Augustine presents as the true history of the City of God against which, and only against which, the history of the City of Man, including the history of Rome, can be properly understood. The work is too long and at times, particularly in the last books, too discursive to make entirely satisfactory reading today, but it remains impressive as a whole and fascinating in its parts. The stinging attack on paganism in the first books is memorable and effective, the encounter with Platonism in books 8–10 is of great philosophical significance, and the last books (especially book 19, with a vision of true peace) offer a view of human destiny that would be widely persuasive for at least a thousand years. In a way, Augustine's *City of God* is (even consciously) the Christian rejoinder to Plato's *Republic* and Cicero's imitation of Plato, his own *Republic*. *City of God* would be read in various ways throughout the Middle Ages, at some points virtually as a founding document for a political order of kings and popes that Augustine could hardly have imagined. At its heart is a powerful contrarian vision of human life, one which accepts the place of disaster, death, and disappointment while holding out hope of a better life to come, a hope that in turn eases and gives direction to life in this world.

RECONSIDERATIONS

In many ways no less unusual a book than his *Confessions*, the *Retractationes* (426–427; *Reconsiderations*), written in the last years of his life, offers a retrospective rereading of Augustine's career. In form, the book is a catalog of his writings with comments on the circumstances of their composition and with the retractions or rectifications he would make in hindsight. (One effect of the book was to make it much easier for medieval readers to find and identify authentic works of Augustine, and this was surely a factor in the remarkable survival of so much of what he wrote.) Another effect of the book is to imprint even more deeply on readers Augustine's own views of his life. There is very little in the work that is false or inaccurate, but the shaping and presentation make it a work of propaganda. The Augustine who emerges has been faithful, consistent, and unwavering in his doctrine and life. Many who knew him would have seen instead either progress or outright desertion, depending on their point of view.

AUGUSTINE'S SPIRIT AND ACHIEVEMENT

Augustine's impact on the Middle Ages cannot be over-estimated. Thousands of manuscripts survive, and many serious medieval libraries—possessing no more than a few hundred books in all—had more works of Augustine than of any other writer. His achievement is paradoxical inas-much as—like a modern artist who makes more money posthumously than in life—most of it was gained after his death and in lands and societies far removed from his own. Augustine was read avidly in a world where Christian orthodoxy prevailed in a way he could barely have dreamed of, hence a world unlike that to which his books were meant to apply.

Some of his success is owed to the undeniable power of his writing, some to his good luck in having maintained a reputation for orthodoxy unblemished even by debates about some of his most extreme views, but, above all, Augustine found his voice in a few themes which he espoused eloquently throughout his career. When he asks himself in his early *Soliloquies* what he desires to know, he replies, "Two things only, God and the soul." Accordingly, he speaks of his reverence for a God who is remote, distant, and mysterious as well as powerfully and unceasingly present in all times and places. *"Totus ubique"* was Augustine's oft-repeated mantra for this doctrine, "The whole of him everywhere."

At the same time, Augustine captures the poignancy and tentativeness of the human condition, centred on the isolated and individual experience of the person. For all he writes of the Christian community, his Christian stands alone before God and is imprisoned in a unique body and soul painfully aware of the different way he knows himself and knows—at a distance and with difficulty—other people.

But Augustine achieves a greater poignancy. His isolated self in the presence of God is denied even the satisfaction of solipsism: the self does not know itself until God deigns to reveal to human beings their identity, and even then no confidence, no rest is possible in this life. At one point in the *Confessions* the mature bishop ruefully admits that "I do not know to what temptation I will surrender next"—and sees in that uncertainty the peril of his soul unending until God should call him home. The soul experiences freedom of choice and ensuing slavery to sin but knows that divine predestination will prevail.

Thousands upon thousands of pages have been written on Augustine and his views. Given his influence, he is often canvassed for his opinion on controversies (from the Immaculate Conception of Mary to the ethics of contraception) that he barely imagined or could have spoken to. But the themes of imperial God and contingent self run deep and go far to explain his refusal to accept Manichaean doctrines of a powerful devil at war with God, Donatist particularism in the face of universal religion, or Pelagian claims of human autonomy and confidence. His views on sexuality and the place of women in society have been searchingly tested and found wanting in recent years, but they, too, have roots in the loneliness of a man terrified of his father—or his God.

In the end, Augustine and his own experience, so vividly displayed and at the same time veiled in his *Confessions*, disappear from view, to be replaced by the serene teacher depicted in medieval and Renaissance art. It is worth remembering that Augustine ended his life in the midst of a community that feared for its material well-being and chose to spend his last days in a room by himself, posting on a wall where he could see them the texts of the seven penitential Psalms, to wrestle one last time with his sins before meeting his maker.

ANICIUS MANLIUS SEVERINUS BOETHIUS

Boethius was a Roman scholar, a Christian philosopher, a statesman, and the author of the celebrated *De consolatione philosophiae* (*Consolation of Philosophy*), a largely Neoplatonic work in which the pursuit of wisdom and the love of God are described as the true sources of human happiness. He was born in Rome in 475 and died in Pavia in 524.

The most succinct biography of Boethius, and the oldest, was written by Cassiodorus, his senatorial colleague, who cited him as an accomplished orator who delivered a fine eulogy of Theodoric, king of the Ostrogoths who made himself king of Italy. Cassiodorus also mentioned that Boethius wrote on theology, composed a pastoral poem, and was most famous as a translator of works of Greek logic and mathematics.

Other ancient sources, including Boethius' own *De consolatione philosophiae*, give more details. He belonged to the ancient Roman family of the Anicii, which had been Christian for about a century and of which Emperor Olybrius had been a member. Boethius' father had been consul in 487 but died soon afterward, and Boethius was raised by Quintus Aurelius Memmius Symmachus, whose daughter Rusticiana he married. He became consul in 510 under the Ostrogothic king Theodoric. Although little of Boethius' education is known, he was evidently well trained in Greek. His early works on arithmetic and music are extant, both based on Greek handbooks by Nicomachus of Gerasa, a 1st-century-CE Palestinian mathematician. There is little that survives of Boethius' geometry, and there is nothing of his astronomy.

It was Boethius' scholarly aim to translate into Latin the complete works of Aristotle with commentary and all the works of Plato "perhaps with commentary," to be followed by a "restoration of their ideas into a single harmony." Boethius' dedicated Hellenism, modeled on that of the

Anicius Manlius Severinus Boethius. © Photos.com/Jupiterimages

Roman orator Cicero, supported his long labour of translating Aristotle's *Organon* (six treatises on logic) and the Greek glosses on the work.

Boethius had begun before 510 to translate Porphyry's *Isagoge,* a 3rd-century Greek introduction to Aristotle's logic, and elaborated it in a double commentary. He then translated the *Katēgoriai,* wrote a commentary in 511 in the year of his consulship, and also translated and wrote two commentaries on the second of Aristotle's six treatises, the *Peri hermeneias* ("On Interpretation"). A brief ancient commentary on Aristotle's *Analytika Protera* ("Prior Analytics") may be his too; he also wrote two short works on the syllogism.

About 520 Boethius put his close study of Aristotle to use in four short treatises in letter form on the ecclesiastical doctrines of the Trinity and the nature of Christ; these are basically an attempt to solve disputes that had resulted from the Arian heresy, which denied the divinity of Christ. Using the terminology of the Aristotelian categories, Boethius described the unity of God in terms of substance and the three divine persons in terms of relation. He also tried to solve dilemmas arising from the traditional description of Christ as both human and divine, by deploying precise definitions of "substance," "nature," and "person." Notwithstanding these works, doubt has at times been cast on Boethius' theological writings because in his logical works and in the later *Consolation,* the Christian idiom is nowhere apparent. The 19th-century discovery of the biography written by Cassiodorus, however, confirmed Boethius as a Christian writer, even if his philosophical sources were non-Christian.

In about 520 Boethius became *magister officiorum* (head of all the government and court services) under Theodoric. His two sons were consuls together in 522. Eventually Boethius fell out of favour with Theodoric. The *Consolation* contains the main extant evidence of his fall but does not clearly describe the actual accusation against him. After the healing of a schism between Rome and the church of Constantinople in 520, Boethius and other senators may have been suspected of communicating with the Byzantine emperor Justin I, who was orthodox in faith whereas Theodoric was Arian. Boethius openly defended the senator Albinus, who was accused of treason "for having written to the emperor Justin against the rule of Theodoric." The charge of treason brought against Boethius was aggravated by a further accusation of the practice of magic, or of sacrilege, which the accused was at great pains to reject. Sentence was passed and was ratified by the Senate, probably under duress. In prison, while he was awaiting execution, Boethius wrote his masterwork, *De consolatione philosophiae.*

The *Consolation* is the most personal of Boethius' writings, the crown of his philosophical endeavours. Its style, a welcome change from the Aristotelian idiom that provided the basis for the jargon of medieval Scholasticism, seemed to the 18th-century English historian Edward Gibbon "not unworthy of the leisure of Plato or Tully." The argument of the *Consolation* is basically Platonic. Philosophy, personified as a woman, converts the prisoner Boethius to the Platonic notion of Good and so nurses him back to the recollection that, despite the apparent injustice of his enforced exile, there does exist a *summum bonum* ("highest good"), which "strongly and sweetly" controls and orders the universe. Fortune and misfortune must be subordinate to that central Providence, and the real existence of evil is excluded. Humans have free will, but it is no obstacle to divine order and foreknowledge. Virtue, whatever the appearances, never goes unrewarded. The prisoner is finally consoled by the hope of reparation and reward beyond death. Through the five books of this argument, in which poetry alternates with prose, there is no specifically Christian tenet. It is the creed of a Platonist, though nowhere glaringly incongruous with Christian faith. The most widely read book in medieval times, after the Vulgate Bible, it transmitted the main doctrines of Platonism to the Middle Ages. The modern reader may not be so readily consoled by its ancient modes of argument, but he may be impressed by Boethius' emphasis on the possibility of other grades of Being beyond the one humanly known and of other dimensions to the human experience of time.

After his detention, probably at Pavia, he was executed in 524. His remains were later placed in the church of San Pietro in Ciel d'Oro in Pavia, where, possibly through a confusion with his namesake, St. Severinus of Noricum, they received the veneration due to a martyr and a memorable salute from Dante.

When Cassiodorus founded a monastery at Vivarium, in Campania, he installed there his Roman library and

Anicius Manlius Severinus Boethius, woodcut, 1537. © Photos.com/Jupiterimages

included Boethius' works on the liberal arts in the anno-
tated reading list (Institutiones) that he composed for the
education of his monks. Thus, some of the literary habits
of the ancient aristocracy entered the monastic tradition.
Boethian logic dominated the training of the medieval
clergy and the work of the cloister and court schools. His
translations and commentaries, particularly those of the
Katēgoriai and *Peri hermeneias,* became basic texts in medieval Scholasticism. The great controversy over nominalism
(denial of the existence of universals) and realism (belief in
the existence of universals) was incited by a passage in his
commentary on Porphyry. Translations of the *Consolation*
appeared early in the great vernacular literatures, with
King Alfred (9th century) and Chaucer (14th century) in
English, Jean de Meun (a 13th-century poet) in French, and
Notker Labeo (a monk of around the turn of the 11th
century) in German. There was a Byzantine version in the
13th century by Planudes and a 16th-century English one
by Elizabeth I.

Thus the resolute intellectual activity of Boethius in
an age of change and catastrophe affected later, very different ages; and the subtle and precise terminology of
Greek antiquity survived in Latin when Greek itself was
little known.

CONCLUSION

The ancient philosophers are distinguished as the inventors of philosophy and as the originators of the basic conceptual framework within which Western philosophy has been practiced from the Middle Ages down to the present day. Their most important legacy, however, must be their conviction that human beings are capable on their own of understanding the deepest mysteries of the universe and of human existence and that the proper road to this achievement is not through religion or magic but through careful empirical observation and the application of reason. A related belief, characteristic of most ancient Greek philosophy, is that this kind of rational investigation is worthwhile and important not merely because it satisfies human beings' natural intellectual curiosity but because it makes human life richer and more meaningful through the understanding and wisdom that it yields. Socrates' dictum "the unexamined life is not worth living" is a famous example of this attitude as it applies to reflection on individual moral character.

These assumptions have not been shared by all Western societies in all ages, of course, and even today they are questioned or dismissed in some segments of Western intellectual and religious culture. In this respect these venerable intellectual ideals are still not secure; indeed, some more pessimistic thinkers have argued that they are in peril. Lest they be lost or forgotten altogether, therefore, we would do well to remember the profound thinkers of ancient philosophy.

acousmatic Members of a group of followers of Pythagoras.

akrasia Moral weakness, wherein one acts against what one knows to be morally right.

apeiron According to Anaximander, the infinite and indefinite source of the physical world.

aporia The state of being at a loss, often expressed by the interlocutors of Socrates in the dialogues of Plato.

atomism Belief that small indivisible and indestructible particles form the basis of the entire universe.

demagoguery The practice of exploiting popular sentiments and prejudices in order to gain political power.

doxa Belief or opinion, as opposed to knowledge.

elenchos Technique of testing of putative experts involving questioning issues suitably related to the expert's original claim.

encomium An expression of praise or admiration.

epistemology The study of the nature, origin, and limits of human knowledge.

eristic One who partakes in argument or dispute.

ethics Philosophical discipline that addresses morality and questions of right and wrong, good and bad.

exegesis Critical examination or analysis of a text, especially of Scripture.

henad According to the Neoplatonists, an expression or manifestation of the unifying power of the One identified with a particular pagan god.

homily A discourse on religious or moral themes delivered during the course of a church service.

hoplite Ancient Greek infantry soldier outfitted with heavy armour.

hylozoism Philosophical belief system that views all matter as living.

isonomy Equality or equilibrium.

Logos An ordering principle that gives the cosmos meaning and structure and serves as mediator between the divine and physical world.

metaphysics The philosophical study of the ultimate nature of reality.

nous The human faculty of intellectual apprehension or a transcendent or divine intellect or organizing principle; according to Plotinus it is the first creation of the One.

ontology The metaphysical study of the nature of existence or being.

Peripatetic A student at the Lyceum, the school founded by Aristotle.

putative Commonly viewed as or supposed.

rhapsodist A singer who recited poetry in ancient Greece.

sensible particular An object that can be perceived through one or more of the senses.

solipsism Theory that the self is capable of knowing only itself or that the self alone is real.

sophistry Misleading argumentation meant to deceive others.

syllogistic System of logical inference from whole declarative statements, originally developed by Aristotle.

syncretism The fusion of varying belief systems.

teleological Concerning explanation by appeal to purpose, goal, design, or function.

theurgy The practice of certain rituals or methods, sometimes deemed magical in nature, designed to persuade supernatural powers to intervene on behalf of humans.

trinitarian Composed of three parts.

trope Figurative use of language.

voluptuary One concerned primarily with luxury and sensual pleasure.

Bibliography

Socrates, Plato, and Aristotle

Overviews of Socrates' life are presented in C.C.W. Taylor, *Socrates* (1998; also reissued as C.C.W. Taylor, R.M. Hare, and Jonathan Barnes, *Greek Philosophers: Socrates, Plato, and Aristotle*, 1999); and Thomas C. Brickhouse and Nicholas D. Smith, *The Philosophy of Socrates* (2000). A large scholarly literature focuses on the seminal work of Gregory Vlastos, including his *Socrates: Ironist and Moral Philosopher* (1991), and his *Socratic Studies* (1994). Discussions of many diverse aspects of the Socrates of Plato's early dialogues are included in Thomas C. Brickhouse and Nicholas D. Smith, *Plato's Socrates* (1994); and Terence Irwin, *Plato's Ethics*, chapters 1–9 (1995), pp. 3–147. Socratic irony is discussed in Alexander Nehamas, *The Art of Living: Socratic Reflections from Plato to Foucault* (1998), pp. 19–98. Paul A. Vander Waerdt (ed.), *The Socratic Movement* (1994), contains many essays on the non-Platonic "Socratic discourses" and the philosophical movements inspired by Socrates in antiquity. An unusual perspective is presented in John Beversluis, *Cross-Examining Socrates: A Defense of the Interlocutors in Plato's Early Dialogues* (2000). Hugh H. Benson, *Socratic Wisdom: The Model of Knowledge in Plato's Early Dialogues* (2000) examines Socratic method and epistemology.

George Grote, *Plato and the Other Companions of Sokrates*, new ed., 4 vol. (1885, reissued 1992), is a venerable study. The order of composition of the dialogues is discussed in Leonard Brandwood, *The Chronology of Plato's Dialogues* (1990). R.B. Rutherford, *The Art of Plato: Ten Essays in Platonic Interpretation* (1995), examines Plato's use of literary elements; while Debra Nails, *The People of Plato* (2002), gives full information on the historical characters on whom Plato's are based.

Good introductory studies of Aristotle's thought include J.L. Ackrill, *Aristotle the Philosopher* (1981, reprinted 1986); Jonathan Barnes, *Aristotle* (1982, reissued 1996; also published as *Aristotle: A Very Short Introduction*, 2000); and W.D. Ross, *Aristotle*, 6th ed. (1995). Two of the most influential books on Aristotle written in the 20th century are Werner W. Jaeger, *Aristotle: Fundamentals of the History of His Development*, 2nd ed. (1948, reissued 1968; originally published in German, 1923); and Harold Cherniss, *Aristotle's Criticism of Plato and the Academy* (1944, reissued 1962). Most scholarly work on Aristotle appears in articles rather than in books. Jonathan Barnes (ed.), *The Cambridge Companion to Aristotle* (1995), is a useful anthology with an extensive bibliography. The proceedings of the triennial *Symposium Aristotelicum* contain some of the most up-to-date work.

The best general biography of Aristotle is Ingemar Düring, *Aristotle in the Ancient Biographical Tradition* (1957, reprinted 1987). The classic study of Aristotle's syllogistic is Jan Lukasiewicz, *Aristotle's Syllogistic from the Standpoint of Modern Formal Logic*, 2nd ed. enlarged (1957, reprinted 1987). An insightful study of Aristotle's metaphysics is Richard Sorabji, *Necessity, Cause, and Blame: Perspectives on Aristotle's Theory* (1980). Amélie Oksenberg Rorty (ed.), *Essays on Aristotle's "Ethics"* (1980, reissued 1996), is a valuable collection of papers. John M. Cooper, *Reason and Human Good in Aristotle* (1975, reprinted 1986), also is important. Other notable works are Anthony Kenny, *The Aristotelian Ethics: A Study of the Relationship Between the Eudemian and Nicomachean Ethics of Aristotle* (1978), *Aristotle's Theory of the Will* (1979), and *Aristotle on the Perfect Life* (1992, reissued 1995); Sarah Broadie, *Ethics with Aristotle* (1991); and Richard Kraut, *Aristotle: Political Philosophy* (2002), on Aristotle's politics and ethics.

Classical philosophical influences on early Christianity are discussed in Christopher Stead, *Philosophy in Christian*

Antiquity (1994); and Robert Louis Wilken, *The Spirit of Early Christian Thought* (2003).

HISTORIES

Detailed histories of the whole course of Greek and Roman philosophy can be found in Eduard Zeller, *Die Philosophie der Griechen*, 6th ed., 3 vol. in 6 (1919), also available in English translation from parts of various editions. Equally thorough is the great work by W.K.C. Guthrie, *A History of Greek Philosophy*, 6 vol. (1962–81, reissued 1986). Short introductions to Greek philosophy in English are Margaret E.J. Taylor, *Greek Philosophy* (1921, reissued 1947); Rex Warner, *The Greek Philosophers* (1958, reissued 1986); and the excellent survey by W.K.C. Guthrie, *The Greek Philosophers: From Thales to Aristotle* (1950, reissued 1994). Also valuable are Reginald E. Allen (ed.), *Greek Philosophy: Thales to Aristotle*, 3rd ed. rev. and expanded (1991); and Jason L. Saunders (ed.), *Greek and Roman Philosophy After Aristotle* (1966, reissued 1994).

TEXTS

An influential source from perhaps the 3rd century is Diogenes Laertius, *Lives of Eminent Philosophers*, trans. from the Greek by R.D. Hicks, 2 vol. (1925, reissued 1991). The best comprehensive collection of the fragments of the pre-Socratic philosophers is still Hermann Diels and Walther Kranz, *The Older Sophists: A Complete Translation by Several Hands of the Fragments in Die Fragmente der Vorsokratiker*, ed. by Rosamund Kent Sprague (1972, reissued 2001), made more readily accessible for English-speaking readers by Hermann Diels, *Ancilla to the Pre-Socratic Philosophers*, trans. by Kathleen Freeman (1948, reissued 1983). A good selection of texts is C.J. de Vogel, *Greek Philosophy: A Collection of Texts*, 4th ed. (1969–).

INDEX